CONDUCTING
A WRONGFUL
DISMISSAL
ACTION
1996

David J. Corry,
B.A., M.Sc., LL.B.
of Bennett Jones Verchere, Calgary

James M. Petrie,
B.B.A., LL.B., LL.M.
of Petrie Richmond Goss, Fredericton

CARSWELL
Thomson Professional Publishing

Canadian Cataloguing in Publication Data

Corry, David J., 1954-
Conducting a wrongful dismissal action

(Alberta practice guide. Civil litigation series)
Includes index.
ISBN 0-459-54833-6

1. Employees – Dismissal of – Law and Litigation – Alberta.
2. Actions and defenses – Alberta. I. Petrie, James M. (James
Michael, 1968-   . II. Title. III. Series.

KEA406.2.C67 1996   344.7123'012596   C96-932107-4
KF3471.C67 1996

The publisher is not engaged in rendering legal, accounting or other professional advice. If legal advice or other expert assistance is required, the services of a competent professional should be sought. The analysis contained
herein represents the opinions of the authors and should in no way be con-
strued as being official or unofficial policy of any governmental body.

CARSWELL
Thomson Professional Publishing

SUMMARY TABLE OF CONTENTS

For a detailed Table of Contents, see page ix.

DEDICATION

This book is dedicated to my Father and Mother, Derek and Coral Corry with thanks for their love, guidance, generosity and support throughout their years. May God bless them both.

D.J.C.

To J. Gordon Petrie, Q.C., who continues to inspire me.

J.M.P.

PREFACE

Although my wife, Maureen, and my children, Tonya, Michelle and Ryan will always be my first love in life – close behind is my love of the law. I also love to teach and work with new lawyers interested in labour and employment law. That is why I agreed to write this Practice Guide.

It couldn't have come at a worst time. I was already committed to writing a book on Collective Bargaining and updating the Labour Relations Code Practitioner's Guide. Maureen's tolerance for these projects was understandably growing thin. I therefore could not have undertaken the task without the invaluable assistance of Jamie Petrie who is now articling in New Brunswick.

This book afforded me the opportunity to tell Jamie everything I knew about the area of wrongful dismissal. It is the culmination of my experience accumulated over my years of practice, writing and teaching in labour and employment law. I had hurriedly put my thoughts down – Jamie developed it into a comprehensive, publishable product. I am impressed with what he did and am grateful for it.

I hope that you are able to benefit from the practical guidance that Jamie and I offer you in this Guide. I hope that it assists you in representing your clients more effectively and efficiently. No doubt, as I have, you too will learn some things along the way. I therefore welcome your thoughts and comments so that I can improve the next version if I am given the privilege to prepare another one.

This is only a Guide, and therefore I encourage you to take the suggestions that we mention together with your own research and insight to the law. This is a forever changing field. With changes to the legislation, developments in the jurisprudence, and changes in the business practice, the law of wrongful dismissal is continually evolving. Practical guidance will change along with it. I hope that this Guide will a useful start for you and that your continuing study of this area of law will provide the rest.

If you are a new lawyer in the area of wrongful dismissal, I suggest that the Guide be read in its entirety. That will give an overview of the area of wrongful dismissal from the first consultation with the client through to the end of the appeal process and wrapping up the file. Thereafter, the relevant sections of the Guide can be referred to from time to time.

Whatever approach you choose, I hope that the Guide is helpful to you.

I should also like to thank my assistant, Colleen Werenka, for her assistance in typing, and for the assistance of Elaine Balestra, the Manager of our Document Processing Department, and all of her staff who assisted on this project. Without their invaluable assistance neither this nor any of the other extensive books that I have worked on would ever have been published.

David J. Corry
January 1997

TABLE OF CONTENTS

Chapter 3
REPRESENTING EMPLOYERS

Chapter 4
SPECIAL PRACTICE ISSUES

Chapter 5
DISCOVERY

Chapter 6
GETTING READY

Chapter 7
NEGOTIATIONS AND SETTLEMENT

Chapter 8
PREPARATION FOR TRIAL

Chapter 9
THE CONDUCT OF THE TRIAL

Chapter 10
POST-TRIAL MATTERS

Chapter 11
INCOME TAX CONSIDERATIONS

Chapter 12
APPEAL

TABLE OF CONCORDANCE

The *Employment Standards Code*, S.A. 1988, c. E-10.2, has been repealed and substituted by the *Employment Standards Code*, S.A. 1996, c. E-10.3, which Act has received Royal Assent, but has not yet been proclaimed in force. The following is a concordance of those sections of the *Employment Standards Code*, S.A. 1988, c. E-10.2, mentioned within this Practice Guide, with the corresponding sections of the *Employment Standards Code*, S.A. 1996, c. E-10.3, to be used when the latter Act has been proclaimed in force.

Employment Standards Code

S.A. 1988, c. E-10.2	S.A. 1996, c. E-10.3
s. 11	s. 5
Pt. II, Divs. 5, 7 & 8	Pt. 2, Divs. 3 to 6
s. 57	ss. 55, 56
s. 58	s. 55(2)
s. 58(1)(e)	s. 55(2)(a)
ss. 92-102	ss. 82-94
s. 98	s. 90

At the time of publication, the *Limitation of Actions Act*, R.S.A. 1980, c. L-15, has been repealed and substituted by S.A. 1996, c. L-15.1, which Act has also not yet been proclaimed in force.

1

OVERVIEW OF
WRONGFUL DISMISSAL ACTION

1.1 SCOPE OF GUIDE

This practice guide covers common law wrongful dismissal actions and applies to non-union employees or union employees who are not governed by a collective agreement. Union employees covered by a collective agreement must resort to the grievance and arbitration process: *Weber v. Ontario Hydro* (1995), [1995] 2 S.C.R. 929; *St. Anne Nackawic Pulp & Paper Co. v. C.P.U., Loc. 219* (1986), [1986] 1 S.C.R. 704; *Oliva v. Strathcona Steel* (1986), 48 Alta. L.R. (2d) 193 (C.A.), leave to appeal to S.C.C. refused (1987), 50 Alta. L.R. (2d) xlvii.

1.2 WHO MAY SUE FOR WRONGFUL DISMISSAL

1.2.1 NATURE OF ACTION

o The law of wrongful dismissal applies to "employees". At common law, all employees are covered by either an oral or a written contract of employment. Most contracts are of an indefinite duration, in which case the law implies that the employer is obligated to provide reasonable notice of termination of employment unless there is just cause for summary dismissal. The common law of dismissal may not be directly applicable to employees who have entered into fixed-term contracts of employment or where the contract specifies the amount to be paid upon termination. (See: *Lambert v. Canadian Assn. of Optometrists* (1994), 6 C.C.E.L. (2d) 129 (Ont. Gen. Div.), affirmed (1996), 19 C.C.E.L. (2d) 315 (Ont. C.A.); *Hodgson v. Sun Valley Co-op Ltd.* (1991), 38 C.C.E.L. 281 (Man. Q.B.)).

o Past cases have held that agents and independent contractors were presumed to be dismissible at will unless there was an express or implied contractual term to the contrary.

o The law applies a series of tests in order to distinguish "employees" from "agents" and "independent contractors". The court examines all elements of the relationship between the parties including control, ownership of tools, chance of profit and risk of loss, integration and economic dependency. (See: *Jaremko v. A.E. LePage Real Estate Services Ltd.* (1989), 69 O.R. (2d) 323 (C.A.); *Walden v. Danger Bay Productions Ltd.* (1994), 90 B.C.L.R. (2d) 180 (C.A.)).

o This distinction between employees, independent contractors and agents has become less important as courts have been more willing to recognize "employment-like" relationships and have applied the same dismissal rights as to full employees. (See: *Montreal (City) v. Montreal Locomotive Works Ltd.* (1946), [1947] 1 D.L.R. 161 (P.C.); *Boettcher v. Stremecki* (1980), 25 A.R. 372 (Q.B.).; *R. v. Mac's Milk Ltd.* (1973), 40 D.L.R. (3d) 714 (Alta. C.A.); *Talbot v. Pan Ocean Corp.* (1980), 109 D.L.R. (3d) 172 (Alta. Q.B.)).

1.2.2   CHECKLIST TO DETERMINE INDEPENDENT CONTRACTOR/EMPLOYEE STATUS

o If a majority of the following items apply then the party could be hired as an independent contractor:

  o The company does not instruct about when, where and how work is to be performed (i.e., the contractor controls the work, not the company).

  o The service is not an integral part of the company's operations.

  o The service does not have to be rendered by the independent contractor personally (i.e., the contractor can chose its own employees to carry out the contract).

  The independent contractor hires, supervises and pays assistants or its own employees.

2

The relationship is not continuing.

The company does not set fixed hours.

Part-time work is not required.

The work is done off the company's premises. The company does not set the order or sequence of work.

No written or oral reports are required.

Payment is not by the hour, week or month, but by function or job.

The contractor has a GST number and adds GST to the invoice.

The company does not pay any expenses of the independent contractor except those directly incurred in performing the contract.

The company does not furnish tools and materials.

The independent contractor has an investment in equipment used or in premises used for service performed for the company (i.e., the risk of profit or loss is with the contractor).

The independent contractor works for other companies and persons as well. The independent contractor's service is available to the public.

The independent contractor has its own W.C.B. account and its employees are covered under that account.

o If the majority of these items do not apply, the individual should probably be hired as an employee.

1.2.3 LEGISLATION

o The federal *Canada Labour Code* ("*C.L.C.*"), R.S.C. 1985, c. L-2, and Alberta's *Employment Standards Code* ("*E.S.C.*"), S.A. 1988, c. E-10.2,[1] contain provisions which set out a minimum period of written notice or an amount of pay in lieu of notice which must be given to an employee prior to termination of employment (*C.L.C.*, s. 230; *E.S.C.*, s. 57). The statutes do not affect an employee's right to pursue a common law remedy which in most cases provides for greater notice than that set out in the statute.

---

[1] This Act has been repealed and substituted by the *Employment Standards Code*, S.A. 1996, c. E-10.3, which has not yet been proclaimed. See Table of Concordance, p. xxi, for equivalent sections in new Act.

o Employment standards legislation also sets out minimum standards for hours worked, overtime, holiday pay and statutory holidays (*C.L.C.*, Pt. III; *E.S.C.*, Pt. 2, Divs. 5, 7 and 8). Generally these entitlements are not enforceable at common law unless they form part of the express employment contract. Those entitlements are therefore claimed through the statutory mechanism for recovery (*C.L.C.*, s. 251.1; *E.S.C.*, ss. 92-102).

o However, an employee whose complaint has been dealt with under employment standards legislation may be barred from seeking a civil remedy because of the doctrine of issue estoppel. (See: *Kenney v. Browning-Ferris Industries Ltd.* (1988), 23 C.C.E.L. 264 (Alta. Q.B.); *Sitka Forest Products Ltd. v. Andrew* (1988), 32 B.C.L.R. (2d) 62 (S.C.)).

1.2.4   TERMINATION

o Most employees are hired on an indefinite contract of employment. That is, the contract does not specify a termination date.

o In the case of all indefinite contracts, reasonable notice of termination must be given to an employee unless there is just cause for the termination.

o Where there is a definite term and the employment continues beyond the expiry date, the relationship becomes an indefinite contract of employment. The employee is then entitled to reasonable notice of dismissal absent cause.

o An indefinite contract of employment can be terminated by an employer for any reason upon providing an employee with reasonable notice.

o If there is just cause for dismissal, there is no need to give reasonable notice or severance pay.

o Where an employee has not been given sufficient notice of dismissal, he or she may sue for wrongful dismissal on the ground that the employer did not have just cause or did not provide reasonable notice.

1.3 JUST CAUSE

o An employer may terminate an employment contract for just cause without giving notice to the employee (see: *C.L.C.*, ss. 235, 236; *E.S.C.*, s. 58). The existence of just cause is a question of fact. The employer has the onus of proving just cause at least on a balance of probabilities.

o The issue of whether an employee's actions are serious enough to justify summary dismissal is a question of fact to be assessed in all of the circumstances of each case. This may be more difficult to establish in the case of a long service employee or one who is employed at a more senior level.

o An employee's record of good conduct is carefully considered together with the allegations of cause to determine whether the conduct is out of character.

o Serious misconduct, habitual neglect of duty, gross incompetence, conduct incompatible with fulfillment of his or her duties, conduct prejudicial to the employer's business, or if he or she has been guilty of wilful disobedience to the employer's orders in a matter of substance are grounds for summary dismissal.

o Accumulation of a number of minor incidences can also justify summary dismissal, if it results in a serious deterioration in the business relationship.

o In cases of deteriorated performance, an employer has a duty to warn the employee and give him or her sufficient time to improve performance before summary dismissal.
   o Warnings must be clear and unequivocal.
   o Where performance is an issue, the employer must outline what is expected of the employee and make positive recommendations to facilitate the improvement in the employee's performance.

o Where a period of time has been given for the employee to improve, the employer may be prevented from dismissing the employee for the same problem or incident of misconduct which precipitated the trial period until the period of time has elapsed.

o If an employer condones misconduct or incompetence, it cannot later cite the same misconduct as cause to fire the employee without notice. Condonation, however, only applies where the employer knows of the misconduct. After the employer has knowledge, it is entitled to a period of time in which to decide on an appropriate course of action.

o A personality conflict between employee and employer which does not affect the employee's ability to perform his or her duties, and does not cause undue prejudice to the employer, does not justify the summary dismissal.

o Refusal to accept a reasonable transfer, where transfers are a regular part of the business, will justify termination of employment without notice. However, a pending relocation of employment which is not specified in the employment contract, or which cannot be implied from the nature of the job, may constitute a constructive dismissal. A refusal to transfer under such circumstances will not justify dismissal without notice. See Section 2.4.1, *infra*.

o Chronic lateness or prolonged absence from work are adequate grounds for summary dismissal in most circumstances. However, isolated absence or occasional lateness will not justify summary dismissal.

o Redundancy of an employee's position, economic difficulties of an employer, and corporate reorganization, do not constitute grounds for dismissal without notice.

o Misconduct outside work will not generally justify dismissal without notice unless the employee's conduct is totally incompatible with the proper discharge of his or her duties, or has caused severe prejudice to the employer.

o Illness of a temporary nature will not constitute just cause for dismissal. An employer who dismisses an employee who is temporarily ill or disabled may be in violation of the Alberta or federal human rights legislation which prohibits discrimination on the ground of a physical or mental disability. See: *Human Rights, Citizenship and Multiculturalism Act*, R.S.A. 1980, c. H-11.7, s. 7; *Canadian Human Rights Act*, R.S.C. 1985, c. H-6, ss. 3 and 7.

o An illness of a permanent nature or of long duration under the circumstances constitutes a frustration of the employment contract justifying termination.

1.4 NOTICE OF TERMINATION

1.4.1 FORM OF NOTICE

o An employer may terminate an indefinite contract of employment without cause provided the employee receives reasonable notice or pay in lieu of reasonable notice.

o Notice may take the form of any communication of the employer to the employee that the employee will either immediately, or on the specified date, cease to be employed by the employer.

o In the case of a corporate employer, notice need not be by resolution of the corporation or its directors and may be given by anyone with the authority to terminate the employee.

o Notice of dismissal must be specific, unequivocal, and clearly communicated to the employee if it is to be effective in law, and the onus of proving that notice was given rests upon the employer.

o Warning an employee of possible dismissal does not constitute notice of termination.

o Notice begins when the employee has received proper notice and the date of termination has been provided.

1.4.2   AMOUNT OF NOTICE

o The amount of reasonable notice is a question of fact to be decided with reference to each particular case, having regard to the character of employment, length of service, age of the employee, and the availability of similar employment: *Bardal v. Globe and Mail Ltd.* (1960), 24 D.L.R. (2d) 140 (Ont. H.C.); *MacLeod v. Geoservices North America Ltd.* (1983), 44 A.R. 93 (Q.B.); *Bagby v. Gustavson International Drilling Co.* (1980), 24 A.R. 181 (C.A.).

(a)   Seniority

o Generally employees in senior, high-level or managerial positions, or those in highly-skilled, professional or technical positions will be entitled to a longer notice period than a more junior or less skilled employee. But some cases have recently questioned this approach and it is becoming less important. (See: *Johnston v. Algoma Steel Corp.* (1989), 24 C.C.E.L. 1 (Ont. H.C.); *Lekien v. Interprovincial Steel & Pipe Corp.* (1985), 42 Sask. R. 177 (Q.B.)).

(b)   Length of Service

o The employee's length of service is probably the most important factor to be considered by the courts in assessing notice. However, even short-term employees are entitled to a minimum of two to three months notice.

o Where an employee has been enticed or lured away from a former employer, this will provide for a longer period of notice.

o Where service has been interrupted by a leave of absence or work for another employer, then it will run from the re-hiring, and not continuously.

o Where there has been a transfer or sale of the business, and the employee has been transferred to the purchaser, service is usually regarded as continuous for assessing the period of reasonable notice.

(c) Age

- o Older employees, particularly those over 50 years of age, are entitled to a longer period of notice than younger employees.

(d) Availability of Similar Employment

- o Since the purpose of notice is to enable an employee to secure alternative employment, the availability of similar employment is considered in some cases to be a major factor in determining an appropriate notice period.

(e) Economic Circumstances

- o Where an industry is in recession, it may be more difficult for the employee to find alternative employment and the court will therefore award a longer period of notice.

- o However, this is balanced with consideration of the employer's economic difficulties which may have resulted in layoffs for economic reasons, thereby justifying a shorter period of notice.

(f) Specifically Recruited or Relocated Employee

- o An employee who has relocated for an employer is entitled to a larger award of damages than he or she might otherwise be entitled to.

- o A longer period of notice is required where an employee has given up a secure job to go to a new employer.

(g) Probationary and Part-time Employees

- o A probationary employee may be entitled to little or no notice of termination depending upon the circumstances. See: Section 2.5.2, *infra*.

9

o A part-time employee may be entitled to less notice than a full time employee.

(h)   Industry Standards

o Where it is customary in an industry to terminate employment on a relatively short period of notice, the courts will likely apply the customary standard. (See: *Molavi v. S.H. Chandler Architect Ltd.* (1984), 54 A.R. 241 (C.A.)).

1.4.3   PURPOSE OF NOTICE

o The object of notice is to give employees a fair opportunity to obtain a new position without leaving them suddenly without means of supporting themselves or their dependants. Damages or compensation in lieu of notice are a substitute for adequate notice and must be calculated from the date of the actual notice of termination.

o Employers are encouraged to make reasonable offers because where notice or pay in lieu is within a reasonable range, employees are more likely to accept them.

1.5   FURTHER REFERENCE

o For further reference regarding the substantive law of wrongful dismissal, see: D. Harris, *Wrongful Dismissal* (Carswell, 1996); 35 C.E.D. (West. 3rd) Title 153 – Wrongful Dismissal.

o For further reference regarding the assessment of reasonable notice in addition to the above, see: E. Mole, *The Wrongful Dismissal Practice Manual* (Butterworths, 1996); H. Levitt, *Law of Dismissal in Canada* (2nd ed.) (Canada Law Book, 1992).

2

REPRESENTING
FORMER EMPLOYEES

2.1 INTRODUCTION

o The goal in representing the former employee in wrongful
dismissal actions is to obtain the necessary background information to evaluate the damages and obtain just compensation in lieu of reasonable notice of dismissal.

o It is usually in the interest of the employee to obtain the
best possible severance package in the shortest period of
time. This is not only because of the practical need to have
sufficient financial resources while attempting to secure alternative employment, but also because of the impact of
mitigation, taxes, unemployment benefit repayment obligations, and legal fees, which diminish over time the net
recovery of the plaintiff.

2.2 INITIAL TELEPHONE INQUIRY

o Initial contact with the former employee is usually by
telephone. The employee has lost his or her job, is facing
an uncertain economic future, and may be understandably
distraught as a result. Legal and practical advice which is
prompt and accurate is needed.

2.2.1   INFORMATION TO GATHER

o In addition to the name, address and telephone number of the client, obtain the name of the employer and ascertain whether there is a conflict in acting for the former employee.

o Obtain very general background facts, including job title and duties, length of service, age, supervisory and professional responsibilities (if any), and a summary of the circumstances leading to termination of employment. Determine if the employee has any immediate plans for future employment and whether the employee has any idea of how long it will take to get another job.

o Confirm that the employee is not represented by a union. Employees represented by a union should contact their union representative and file a grievance as soon as possible. Grievances are subject to very stringent time lines. A grievance may represent the only remedy available to the employee. The collective agreement will have to be reviewed at the first opportunity to advise the client.

o Ask if a final pay cheque was given to the employee and determine what amounts were provided for:

   o salary and wages

   o overtime

   o vacation pay

   o statutory pay in lieu of notice

   o any other pay in lieu of notice

o Ascertain whether any severance offer was made and, if so, determine what the terms are. Caution the client not to accept the severance offer or sign an agreement or general release without the benefit of legal advice.

2.2.2   DETERMINING APPROPRIATE SEVERANCE PAY

o If you have access to a database of wrong dismissal decisions, you may wish to do a preliminary evaluation of the period of reasonable notice and a range of severance. Qualify this as a preliminary evaluation to your client. Explain that this is probably the highest amount that will be recovered as it is subject to the duty to mitigate and depends on whether or not alternative employment has been secured during or after the period of reasonable notice. Advise that a more definitive assessment will be made following the initial interview.

2.2.3   QUALIFYING FOR UNEMPLOYMENT BENEFITS

o Ascertain whether the client has obtained a Record of Employment ("R.O.E."), and whether the client has filed to claim unemployment benefits. If so, provide preliminary advice as to whether the client can expect any problems in qualifying for unemployment benefits.

o *For example, if the employee has left his or her employment voluntarily, or has lost employment as a result of his or her own misconduct, he or she may be disqualified. See: Employment Insurance Act ("E.I.A."), S.C. 1996, c. 23, s. 30.*

o *The circumstances will be reviewed by the commission, which will make a determination. This decision may be appealed to a board of referees, an umpire, and subsequently through to the Federal Court. (See: E.I.A., ss. 114, 115 and 118; Federal Court Act, R.S.C. 1985, c. F-7, s. 28).*

2.2.4   OTHER PRELIMINARY ADVICE

o Advise the client to keep a detailed job search diary, including a résumé, all jobs applied for, copies of letters and applications, any replies, and a log of telephone inquiries for interviews.

o Arrange a convenient time and place for the initial appointment with the client.

o Ask client to bring all relevant documentation to the initial interview, including:
  o the letter of termination of employment and severance package (if any);
  o employment contract;
  o letter of hire;
  o position description pertaining to their former position;
  o evaluations;
  o letters of reference;
  o T-4 slips and draft income tax returns for the last complete year of employment;
  o recent cheque stubs;
  o employee policy and benefit manuals;
  o final pay cheque stub;
  o any other relevant documentation.

2.3   INITIAL CLIENT INTERVIEW

2.3.1   STRUCTURE OF INTERVIEW

o Have the client explain background circumstances leading to termination of employment and why legal advice is being sought.

o Ask questions during and following the client's review to ensure that you have all of the background facts to advise the client and prosecute the case.

o Provide initial legal advice and evaluation, including unemployment benefits and taxation considerations.

o Explain the impact of the duty to mitigate (i.e., that all former employees are under a duty to mitigate their damages by diligently searching for alternative employment), and the need to keep a job search record.

o Outline the steps to be taken prior to and after commencement of litigation.

o Discuss tactical considerations and strategy.

o Reach consensus as to the time and responsibility for the immediate steps to be taken.

2.3.2   INFORMATION TO OBTAIN FROM CLIENT

o Inquire into the factual circumstances leading to the client's termination of employment. Depending on the nature of the case, the information to be obtained from the client generally includes:
  o When was the client hired?
  o Who hired the client?
  o Was the client enticed from secure employment or unemployed at the time?
  o Was the job advertised?
  o What were the details of hiring interview?
  o Were any representations made about the job upon hiring or shortly after?
  o Was there a letter of hire or employment contract?
  o Was there a collective agreement or union in place?

o Review the client's employment history, salary and other remuneration.

o Obtain details of the client's benefits, including pension, pension options following termination, and conversion privileges with respect to life insurance and disability insurance coverage.

o Determine whether there were any job performance reviews or evaluations. If so, review these with the client in detail.

o Determine whether there were any incidents relevant to the client's termination of employment.

o Determine the names of any supervisors and the client's relationship with them.

o Determine the client's relationship with co-workers, customers and clients.

o Determine the circumstance(s) leading to the client's termination of employment and the reasons given by employer for termination of employment.

o Determine whether there was an interview between the client and the employer upon termination of employment and, if so, determine all of the details.

o Determine severance offers or discussions related to severance.

o Examine letters of reference.

o Determine whether the client has applied for unemployment benefits and the response to date.

o Determine whether the client has commenced job search, and if so, examine the job search strategy in detail.

o Make evaluation of job prospects and estimate length of unemployment.

o Review matters of confidentiality and fiduciary duties (if applicable).

o Review the past employer's history with other wrongful dismissal cases. Make an evaluation of the possibility of a negotiated settlement and timing.

2.3.3   DOCUMENTS TO OBTAIN

o The following documents should be reviewed during the initial interview or shortly thereafter:

- o résumé;
- o any job advertisement or posting related to the former position;
- o letter of offer of employment;
- o employment contract;
- o any other signed documents;
- o benefits handbook;
- o benefit and pension statements;
- o T-4 slip and income tax returns;
- o evaluations, commendations and awards;
- o relevant company memoranda and other documents;
- o cheque stubs from last few pay periods, including final cheque stub;
- o letter of termination of employment;
- o severance package;
- o record of employment;
- o job search record, including advertisements for new positions, letters of application, and response letters.

2.3.4 INITIAL ADVICE AND EVALUATION

(a) Common Law and Employment Standards

- o Give an outline of the common law of wrongful dismissal and its relationship to employment standards. Employment standards are minimum standards set out in the applicable provincial and federal statutes; common law is judge-made law.

- o Where no written contract or definite term of employment exists, there will be an implied contract. The implied contract of employment can only be terminated for cause or by reasonable notice.

(b) Cause

- o Outline what constitutes just cause for termination of employment in light of the particular facts of the client's case. See: D. Harris, *Wrongful Dismissal* (Carswell, 1996), §3.10.

17

o Where cause is established, the employer may terminate employment without notice.

o Advise that employer has the onus of establishing just cause and that this is often a difficult onus to meet.

o Provide an initial evaluation as to cause based on the facts disclosed by the client to date and indicate that this evaluation will be updated as the litigation progresses.

(c)   Reasonable Notice

o There is no fixed formula for reasonable notice and the court will make the evaluation based on all of the circumstances of the case including: length of service, position, supervisory or professional responsibilities, age of employee, circumstances leading to termination of employment, possibility of re-employment and so forth. It should be noted that no two cases are alike.

o Evaluation of reasonable notice is based on similar cases reported in Alberta and other jurisdictions.

o Review similar cases and provide initial evaluation by giving a range of reasonable notice periods.

(d)   Duty to Mitigate

o Advise that all former employees are under a duty to mitigate their damages by diligently searching for alternative employment.

o If the employee does not fulfil the duty to mitigate then damages will be reduced by the court.

(e)   Initial Evaluation of Damages

o Make an initial evaluation of the range of damages based on the period of reasonable notice and ensure that this includes damages for loss of compensation and benefits.

Provide the client with a low and a high range estimate, including the following:

o unpaid salary, wages or commissions;
o salary and other remuneration;
o non-discretionary bonuses;
o stock options and other incentive plans;
o compensation for loss of benefits;
o job search expenses;
o other damages.

o See: Harris, *supra*, §4.0.

(f) Impact of New Employment

o Advise that damages are reduced once new employment is commenced.
  o This includes working for another employer, whether the employee or consultant has received remuneration or not, if it is expected that remuneration would normally be paid.
  o This also includes income (or reasonable income expected) obtained through self-employment.
  o This does not include a second job, investment income or self-employment where this pre-dates the termination of employment.

o A court will either reduce damages by income earned during the period of reasonable notice or limit the damages to the period of unemployment. See: Harris, *supra*, §4.75.

2.3.5 JOB SEARCH RECORD

o Given the duty to mitigate and the impact on the assessment of damages, advise the client to diligently search for new employment and keep a job search record. The job search record should consist of:

o a résumé;
o clippings or photocopies of jobs applied for;

19

- o letters of application;
- o details pertaining to any interviews attended, inquiries made or follow up;
- o response letters from potential employers;
- o if employment is obtained, then the details of the job, when it commenced, salary and other remuneration, benefits, etc.

2.3.6   INITIAL *E.I.A.* CONSIDERATIONS

- o Make an initial evaluation as to whether a client will be entitled to unemployment benefits and the impact on his or her wrongful dismissal claim.

- o The initial evaluation should include:
  - o An assessment as to whether the client left the employment voluntarily or as a result of his or her own wilful misconduct. If it is the latter, then the client most likely will not be eligible for unemployment benefits.
  - o A determination of whether the client worked the requisite number of weeks to qualify for unemployment benefits.
  - o A determination of whether the client is entitled to maternity or sickness and disability benefits under the *E.I.A.*.
  - o A review of the Record of Employment ("R.O.E.").
  - o An outline of the procedure for application for unemployment benefits and possible appeals.

- o Determine whether the client will require legal assistance and advice.

- o Advise the client of impact of wrongful dismissal settlement on unemployment benefits. See: Section 2.9.1, *infra*.

2.3.7   FINANCIAL CONSIDERATIONS, LEGAL FEES AND COSTS

- o Review the client's financial circumstances to determine the legal fee arrangement.

o Given the client's unemployment and future uncertainty, it may be inappropriate to charge a retainer fee and bill out regularly for legal fees. In this case, the following options are available:

o Billing upon conclusion of settlement or payment of judgment.

o Placing the client on a budget plan of affordable monthly retainers with the payment of the final amount owing upon conclusion of the matter.

o Entering a contingency fee agreement. However, if there is no issue as to cause and a quick resolution is likely, this may be inappropriate and more costly.

o Fully discuss the method of calculation of legal fees, disbursements and other charges so that the client is comfortable.

o Encourage the client to discuss any concerns regarding legal fees with you.

o Advise the client as to his or her right to have the bill taxed by a taxation officer if there is any serious disagreement that cannot be resolved.

Note: It is a prudent practice to provide all clients with a copy of the Law Society of Alberta brochure, "Understanding Your Lawyer's Fee".

o With respect to costs, advise the client that at the time judgement is given, the court will normally award party and party costs to the successful litigant.

o Advise as to the nature of party and party costs and that these are only a partial indemnity for the legal fees actually expended; higher costs are only awarded in very special cases.

o Advise that solicitor and client costs are only awarded in rare circumstances where a written contract provides for it or the employer's conduct has been so high-handed that the court feels an unusual award of costs is warranted.

o If wrongful dismissal action is dismissed then client likely liable for employer party and party costs.

2.3.8 LEGAL PROCEDURE AND TIME

o Outline to the client the legal procedure and estimated time for each step in a wrongful dismissal claim, including:

   o The time to prepare, review and send the employer a demand letter. Agree on a reasonable time for a response.
   o The time to prepare, review and file a statement of claim.
   o Advise that the employer officially has 15 days to prepare and file a statement of defence. However, this deadline is normally extended as a matter of professional courtesy and ethical obligation between legal counsel for a reasonable time period.
   o Advise as to what is involved in the production of documents and assembling, preparing and filing an affidavit on production. Recommend preparing a draft affidavit on production for review by the client and forwarding producible documents with a draft affidavit to the opposing counsel. The final affidavit for filing can be prepared at the meeting with the client in preparation for examination for discovery or after the examination for discovery (if the opposing counsel agrees).
   o Advise on the preparation and procedure of examination for discovery, and estimate the time until discovery is scheduled and completed.
   o Advise as to the procedure for setting a matter down for trial and estimate the time in which that can be reasonably completed.
   o Advise as to trial procedure and estimate the time when the trial can be completed.

Note: It is a prudent practice to provide the client with a copy of the Law Society of Alberta brochure on "Civil Actions: The Process If You Sue or If You Are Being Sued".

2.3.9 TACTICAL CONSIDERATIONS AND STRATEGY

o In most cases, it is in the employee's best interest to move quickly provided that this does not compromise the employee's ability to obtain a reasonable settlement.

o In some cases, where the employee has a reasonable rapport with a supervisor or senior officer of the company, it may be appropriate to encourage further discussion between the employee and management to see if a suitable settlement can be obtained. Legal counsel can provide their client with background advice as to entitlement and some legal precedent materials for review during those meetings.

o In most cases where legal counsel has been retained by the employee, it is appropriate to begin with a letter to the employer briefly outlining the client's claim and making a without prejudice proposal for settlement. This will often generate fruitful discussions as to settlement. See: Appendix 2B – Sample Demand Letter.

o Usually a brief period (i.e., approximately seven days) is given to resolve matters following delivery of the demand letter. If that is not successful, then a statement of claim should be drafted, issued, and served as soon as possible.

o If a lawyer has been retained by the employer at this point, the statement of claim can be sent to the opposing counsel, provided that he or she admits service and undertakes to file a defence or demand of notice in due course. Otherwise, the statement of claim should be served on the employer pursuant to the Alberta *Rules of Court*. In the case of a corporate employer, this is usually by single registered mail. See: Alberta *Rules of Court*, R. 15; *Business Corporations Act*, S.A. 1981, c. B-15, s. 247.

o Counsel for the former employee should always be striving to move the litigation along through early completion of the production of documents, early scheduling and timely completion of the examinations for discovery, and setting the matter down for trial as quickly as possible.

o When the former employee obtains new employment, then the case will have to be re-evaluated at that time and this may lead to immediate settlement discussions. For example, income from new employment may reduce the damages so significantly that the parties are able to agree on a precise calculation of damages. In most cases, where there is no issue as to cause, this should enable legal counsel to settle the matter. If not, then the employee should consider filing a formal offer of settlement.

2.4   SPECIAL CASES

2.4.1   CONSTRUCTIVE DISMISSAL

o An employee may have a cause of action for constructive dismissal where the employer unilaterally changes a fundamental term or condition of employment without notice or the employee's consent.

o An employer cannot unilaterally alter a fundamental term or condition of employment without providing reasonable notice to the employee or obtaining the employee's consent. Once that occurs, the employee has one of three options:

1. Resigning from employment and suing the employer for constructive dismissal;

2. Protesting the changes and continuing in the job under protest while suing for damages. In most cases, however, the employer will terminate an employee who commences legal action while still employed.

3. Accept the change by either express agreement or by working under the new terms and conditions and taking no further action. In this case the employee will either be deemed to have impliedly accepted the change or may have waived his right to sue for constructive dismissal.

o A minor or incidental change in a term or condition of employment does not give rise to constructive dismissal since the employment contract continues to exist: *Poulos v. Murphy Oil Co.* (1990), 75 Alta. L.R. (2d) 49 (Q.B.); *Hamilton & Olsen Surveys Ltd. v. Otto,* (1993), 12 Alta. L.R. (2d) 431 (C.A.), leave to appeal to S.C.C. refused (1994), 15 Alta. L.R. (3d) lii.

o Therefore, a lateral transfer of an employee from one position in an organization to another, or a corporate re-organization giving rise to a change in duties and reporting structure will not constitute a constructive dismissal because the employment contract has not been fundamentally altered. However, a fundamental change in the duties of an employee will constitute a constructive dismissal when the employee is demoted, or when the duties are so significantly altered that it goes to the very root of the employment contract. Courts have sometimes had difficulty determining whether a change is fundamental resulting in inconsistent decisions in this area. See: *Adams v. Comark Inc.* (1992), 81 Man. R. (2d) 119 (C.A.); *Pottelberg v. British Columbia Telephone Co.* (1995), 11 C.C.E.L. (2d) 87 (B.C.S.C.); *Islip v. Northmount Food Services Ltd.* (1988), 20 C.C.E.L. 250 (B.C.C.A.).

o A significant reduction in remuneration or a change in the manner of compensation that significantly alters the amount of salary and benefits, will constitute a constructive dismissal. This could include the introduction of the new compensation package, changing from salary to straight commission, or a significant reduction in the hours of work. However, a reduction in the benefits package may not constitute constructive dismissal (see: *Hamilton & Olsen Surveys, supra.*

o A forced geographical transfer, if not bargained for at the beginning of employment, or if it is not implied because it is not a customary practice in the particular industry, will constitute a constructive dismissal. It is often implied where an employee is part of a national or international corporation and transfers are reasonably common. On the other hand, if it is clear that the employee was hired to work in a particular location and the transfer would involve a demotion or undue burden or hardship, it may constitute a constructive dismissal.

o A superior's persistent criticisms of an employee's work without cause may constitute a constructive dismissal. Particularly, where the employee is given no assistance in dealing with the superior or in relocating despite frequent requests for help. See: *Paitich v. Clarke Institute of Psychiatry* (1990), 30 C.C.E.L. 235 (Ont. C.A.); see also: D. Harris, *Wrongful Dismissal* (Carswell, 1996), §§3.3 to 3.5.

(a) Condonation

o An employer may implement temporary changes in the conditions of employment on a short-term basis.

o Even where changes may amount to a constructive dismissal, where an employee continues to work under the terms and conditions for an extended period of time without objection, they will be deemed to have waived their right to sue for constructive dismissal. See: *Mosher v. Twin Cities Co-operative Dairy Ltd.* (1984), 63 N.S.R. (2d) 252 (S.C.); *Stephens v. Morris Rod Weeder Co.* (1989), 76 Sask. R. 20 (Q.B.).

(b) Options

o Where it is uncertain whether there is a constructive dismissal or not, the safer option is to advise the employee to clearly object to the change in writing and consider remaining in their employment and suing for damages. However, the employer may react to the lawsuit by terminating the employee.

o In clear cases of constructive dismissal, as the employment contract has been repudiated by the employer's unilateral change, the employee has the option to either resign and sue for constructive dismissal, or remain in his or her employment and sue for the reduction in income or the value of benefits as damages.

(c) Practical Considerations

o Given the uncertainty in some constructive dismissal cases, the employee should set out his or her objections in writing, requesting the employer to remedy the situation by a certain date. If that does not resolve the matter to the employee's satisfaction, the employee can then consider the option of remaining in the employment or leaving.

o Obviously, if the circumstances are intolerable, this may force the employee to leave.

o In a large organization, the safer option may be for the employee to remain in employment and sue for damages.

2.4.2 RESIGNATION

o If an employee voluntarily resigns, this will terminate the contract of employment. If an employee's offer of resignation is not accepted as offered, its acceptance on different terms is not binding on the employee and does not terminate the employment. Under the *Employment Standards Code* (*"E.S.C."*), S.A. 1988, c. E-10.2, s. 57, an employer must provide minimum statutory notice of termination of employment. Under the common law, employees are required to give reasonable notice of termination. See: *Tree Savers International v. Savoy* (1991), 81 Alta. L.R. (2d) 325 (Q.B.), varied (1992), 84 Alta. L.R. (2d) 384 (C.A.).

o A forced resignation amounts to a wrongful dismissal. This includes providing the employee with the option to either resign or be fired.

o If an employee resigns as a result of a loss of temper, or had clearly not intended to resign under the circumstances, it will not constitute a resignation at law (see: *Assouline v. Ogivar Inc.* (1991), 39 C.C.E.L. 100 (B.C.S.C.)). A resignation is void where the employee is mentally incompetent or suffering from an illness and does not understand the consequences of his or her actions. See: *Cranston v. Canadian Broadcasting Corp.* (1994), 2 C.C.E.L. (2d) 301 (Ont. Gen. Div.); *Ewasiuk v. Estevan Area Home Care District 9 Inc.* (1985), 9 C.C.E.L. 267 (Sask. Q.B.).

2.4.3 ILLNESS AND DISABILITY

o A permanent illness that totally precludes the employee from performing their employment, and where it is very unlikely that the employee will be able to return to work, frustrates the employment contract. However, a temporary illness does not. The seriousness of an illness is often difficult to determine.

o An employer who dismisses an employee who is temporarily ill or disabled may also be in violation of the provincial or federal human rights legislation which prohibits discrimination on the ground of a physical or mental disability. See: *Human Rights, Citizenship and Multiculturalism Act* ("*H.R.C.M.A.*"), R.S.A. 1980, c. H-11.7, s. 7; *Canadian Human Rights Act*, R.S.C. 1985, c. H-6, ss. 3 and 7. There is also a duty to accommodate ill or disabled employees unless it amounts to an undue hardship. See: *Central Alberta Dairy Pool v. Alberta (Human Rights Commission)* (1990), [1990] 2 S.C.R. 489.

o Ill or disabled employees may also be entitled to disability benefits, either from the employer or through an insurance carrier. Where disability benefits have been improperly terminated or denied, either the employer, the insurance carrier, or both could be liable. See generally: D'Andrea, Corry and Forester, *Illness and Disability in the Workplace* (Canada Law Book, 1996).

2.4.4 EMPLOYEE DISHONESTY

o Where an employee has been dishonest, it will justify dismissal; however, the employer has a heavy onus of proving dishonesty. Mere suspicion of dishonesty or poor judgment will not be enough. See: *Aspinall v. Mid-West Collieries Ltd.* (1926), [1926] 3 D.L.R. 362 (Alta. C.A.); *Meszaros v. Simpson-Sears Ltd.* (1979), 19 A.R. 239 (Q.B.).

o Where the employer's actions amount to defamation, the employee may be able to combine a wrongful dismissal and defamation action. See: *Bailey v. Ventin* (1993), 93 C.L.L.C. 14,030 (Ont. Gen. Div.); *Jonas v. R. Reininger & Sons Ltd.* (1992), 55 O.A.C. 178 (Div. Ct.); *Stadler v. Terrace Corp.* (1983), 41 A.R. 587 (Q.B.).

o Also, in cases where the employer has not proven dishonesty or has acted in bad faith, it could result in a higher damages award against them in the form of punitive and aggravated damages, and a requirement to pay solicitor and client legal costs. See: *Francis v. Canadian Imperial Bank of Commerce* (1992), 41 C.C.E.L. 37 (Ont. Gen. Div.), reversed in part (1994), 7 C.C.E.L. (2d) 1 (Ont. C.A.).

2.4.5   SENIOR OFFICERS, DIRECTORS AND SHAREHOLDERS

o Unless the officer or director also has an employment relationship with the corporation, the proper, legal discharge from their position may not constitute a wrongful dismissal. Thus, they must clearly establish an employment relationship to sue for wrongful dismissal. See: *McGuire v. Wardair Canada Ltd.* (1969), 71 W.W.R. 705 (Alta. T.D.).

o In some cases, an employee may also be a shareholder. If the actions of the employer constitute oppression under the Alberta or Canada *Business Corporations Act*, this may also give rise to an oppression action. See: Alberta *Business Corporations Act*, S.A. 1981, c. B-15, s. 234; *Canada Business Corporations Act*, R.S.C. 1985, c. C-44, s. 241.

2.4.6   HUMAN RIGHTS

o Where the employer's conduct amounts to discrimination contrary to provincial or federal human rights legislation, it may also give rise to a complaint under the applicable legislation. This includes discrimination on the ground of race, religious beliefs, colour, gender, sexual harassment, physical disability, mental disability, marital status, age, ancestry, place of origin, family status or source of income.

o A human rights complaint gives rise to a statutory remedy which is totally separate from the common law remedies for wrongful dismissal. See: *H.R.C.M.A.*.

2.4.7   WRITTEN EMPLOYMENT CONTRACT

o All written employment contracts must be carefully reviewed to ascertain the employee's cause of action. If the employee has been discharged at the end of the term, or in accordance with the notice provisions set out in the contract, and the contract is enforceable, the employee is not entitled to damages in lieu of reasonable notice. See: *Pierce v. Krahn* (1979), 10 Alta. L.R. (2d) 49 (T.D.); *Toronto-Dominion Bank v. Wallace* (1983), 41 O.R. (2d) 161 (C.A.); *Aldo Ippolito & Co. v. Canada Packers Inc.* (1986), 14 C.C.E.L. 76, additional reasons (1986), 14 C.C.E.L. 76 at 89 (Ont. C.A.).

o In the absence of a contractual arrangement, the employee is entitled to reasonable notice. The employee must have expressly agreed to any contrary provision and an employer cannot unilaterally deprive an employee of his common law right to notice by providing it in its personnel manual.

o If a contract of employment provides that the employment can be terminated at any time by either party, with or without cause, the employee is still entitled to reasonable notice if the contract does not provide for termination upon a specified period of notice.

o Where the contract does not provide for at least the minimum notice set out in the *Employment Standards Code, supra*, the clause will be void for illegality. See: *Machtinger v. HOJ Industries Ltd.* (1992), [1992] 1 S.C.R. 986 (S.C.C.).

o The courts may not enforce the contract where:
   o it is harsh or unconscionable, signed under duress, or so unreasonable as to amount to a penalty. That could be the case with both unreasonably low or high notice provisions;

o where the employment contract provides for termination upon less notice than the minimum standards set out in the employment standards legislation;

o where it was not the clear intention of the parties that the provisions have legal effect (i.e., such as in a policy manual);

o where the terms and conditions are set out in a standard form contract which was never actually agreed to, does not cover the whole agreement of the parties, or that is inappropriate in the context of the job.

o where the contract was not presented to the employee at the time of hiring and was unilaterally imposed after the employee had accepted and commenced the job. See *Ryshpan v. Burns Fry Ltd.* (1995), 10 C.C.E.L. (2d) 235 (Ont. Gen. Div.), affirmed (1996), 20 C.C.E.L. (2d) 104 (Ont. C.A.).

2.5   TYPE OF EMPLOYEE

2.5.1   VOLUNTEER EMPLOYEE

o Where all of the circumstances suggest that a person, who expects remuneration, should normally be paid for the work performed, the person working will be an employee. Whether the person is an employee or a volunteer will be determined by the clear intentions of the parties looking at all of the circumstances.

o Where there is a dispute as to whether or not the worker is a volunteer or an employee, the employee may have a cause of action to recover wages based on a *quantum meruit* claim. See: G.H.L. Fridman, *Restitution* (2nd ed.) (Carswell, 1992), pp. 285-98.

2.5.2   PROBATIONARY EMPLOYEE

o A probationary employee is one who agrees with the employer to serve a term of probation during which the employer will provide the employee with the training required and will determine whether the employee is suitable for the job. The probationary status must be agreed to either orally or in writing. The fact that an employee has been recently hired does not mean that he or she is on probation.

o For an employee to be probationary, it must be clear at the time of hiring that he or she is being hired on a probationary basis. Being advised that his or her performance will be reviewed at a certain date does not mean that the employee is on probation until the review date. Further, employment standards legislation does not automatically create a three-month probationary period at common law. See: *Doyle v. Auld* (1990), 33 C.C.E.L. 95 (P.E.I.T.D.); *Davidson v. Lee Valley Tools Ltd.* (1987), [1987] B.C.W.L.D. 725 (S.C.).

o Probationary employees cannot be dismissed at will without sufficient reason. The probationary period is intended to provide the employer with an opportunity to determine the employee's suitability for the job. In order to justify the dismissal of a probationary employee without notice:

  o the employer must act fairly and with reasonable diligence in determining whether or not the proposed employee is suitable for the job;
  o the employee must be given a reasonable opportunity to demonstrate his or her ability to meet the job standards;
  o the job standards must be reasonable.

o In determining the probationary employee's suitability, the employer may consider the employee's character, compatibility with the workplace and the other employees, and the ability to meet present and future job requirements.

o The probationary employee, however, must have received proper training before his or her performance is evaluated.

o The term of probation cannot be extended without express agreement unless there is just cause to extend it.

o A permanent employee cannot be placed on probation without express agreement of the employee or for cause.

2.5.3 GOVERNMENT AND MUNICIPAL EMPLOYEES

o The Alberta government's authority to dismiss at pleasure has been modified by the *Public Service Act*, R.S.A. 1980, c. P-31, s. 25, and the *Public Service Employee Relations Act*, R.S.A. 1980, c. P-33, s. 70.

o In Alberta, employees who are not part of a public service bargaining unit are governed by the *Public Service Act*.

o An employee of a Crown corporation has the status to sue the corporation for wrongful dismissal. See: *Washer v. British Columbia (Toll Highways & Bridges Authority)* (1965), 53 D.L.R. (2d) 620 (B.C.C.A.).

o Municipal employees may sue the municipality as a corporation pursuant to the *Municipal Government Act*, S.A. 1994, c. M-26.1. Some statutory provisions for municipal by-laws provide for a hearing prior to termination. Where this procedure is mandatory, and has not been followed, it may result in reinstatement of the employee upon application for judicial review by the court. If a by-law provides for specific severance allowances, this will usually be followed by the courts.

o Employment and dismissal of police officers is governed by the *Police Act*, S.A. 1988, c. P-12.01.

o The termination of teachers is governed by the *School Act*, S.A. 1988, c. S-3.1.

2.5.4 PART-TIME, CASUAL AND TEMPORARY EMPLOYEES

o Part-time employees are entitled to reasonable notice of dismissal, subject to the same considerations that apply to full-time employees (see: *Davidson v. Worthing* (1986), 2 A.C.W.S. (3d) 212 (B.C.S.C.)). However, a temporary or casual employee, who essentially has the option of selecting the hours worked, is not entitled to reasonable notice (see: *Schwanke v. Para-Med Health Services Inc.* (1985), 9 C.C.E.L. 314 (Alta. Q.B.).

o Foreign employees working in Canada may be entitled to damages for wrongful dismissal. However, they must establish that the corporation carrying on business in Canada is the employer. See: Section 2.6.1 – Multiple Employers.

o Canadian employees who work for a foreign subsidiary or related corporation may be able to establish a sufficient employment relationship with the corporation to sue in Canada.

o Given the uncertainties pertaining to foreign employment, the identity of the employer, and rights upon termination, it is in the employee's best interest to enter into a written employment contract. Where applicable, this contract could be enforceable by arbitration under the *International Commercial Arbitration Act*, S.A. 1986, c. I-6.6. Alternatively, the employee may wish to specify the jurisdiction of governing law and which courts they are prepared to attorn to in their agreements.

2.6   THE EMPLOYER

o In some cases, there may be difficulty ascertaining the true employer or whether there is an employment relationship.

2.6.1   MULTIPLE EMPLOYERS

o Where an employee is transferred to a related corporation, the company having ultimate direction and control over the employee will be the employer. This is often the parent corporation. In cases where both corporations have some control over the employee, both will be an employer. For example, where an employee of a Canadian corporation moved to the United States to establish a U.S. subsidiary, the proper law of the contract was the applicable Canadian province and the true employer was the Canadian company. See: *Bagby v. Gustavson International Drilling Co.*

(1980), 24 A.R. 181 (C.A.); *Campbell v. Pringle & Booth Ltd.* (1988), 30 C.C.E.L. 156 (Ont. H.C.).

2.6.2   SUCCESSORSHIP

o An employment contract is a personal service contract, and is therefore not assignable without the consent of both parties. Upon sale or transfer of a business, the employee's contract automatically terminates unless the employee and the new owner agree to continue employment.

o Where the new owner either expressly or impliedly agrees to continue their employment on the same terms and conditions, the new owner will have assumed the employee's contract, including the obligations as to dismissal. An assignment or novation will be implied where the worker continues to provide services as before which are accepted by the new owner.

o Absent a specific contractual agreement to the contrary, where the new owner subsequently dismisses the employee, in ascertaining the period of reasonable notice the court will account for the employee's entire service to both the predecessor and the successor corporation.

2.6.3   INDEPENDENT CONTRACTORS

o An independent contractor will generally not be entitled to damages for wrongful dismissal. However, if the contract is one of indefinite duration, the independent contractor will be entitled to reasonable notice of termination except for just cause. Otherwise the contract will govern, and the parties need not comply with the minimum notice provisions set out under the employment standards legislation, which is only applicable to employees. See: *E.S.C.*, s. 57.

o The fact that the parties have agreed in writing that a person is an independent contractor is not determinative. The court will look at all of the circumstances of the case to determine the true relationship. See: Section 1.2.2 –

Checklist to Determine Independent Contractor/Employee Status.

2.6.4   RECEIVERSHIP OR BANKRUPTCY

o An assignment in bankruptcy operates as a dismissal from employment.

o The appointment of a receiver/manager by court order or instrument may result in the termination of the contract of employment. Thereafter, if the receiver/manager enters into contracts of employment with the former employees, then the receiver/manager becomes the employer. See: *St. Mary's Paper Inc., Re* (1994), 26 C.B.R. (3d) 273 (Ont. C.A.), affirmed (1996), [1996] 1 S.C.R. 3.

o Upon the appointment of a receiver/manager, there is some doubt as to whether the employee has a right to leave the job and sue for wrongful dismissal. While the court will examine all of the realities of the situation, it would constitute a failure to mitigate where a plaintiff refuses to continue in the same job under the same conditions merely because a receiver/manager has been appointed. See: *Sawarin v. Canadian Acceptance Corp.* (1983), 34 Sask. R. 234 (C.A.).

2.7   ASSESSMENT OF DAMAGES

o The assessment of damages for an employee who has been wrongfully dismissed involves the following steps:

Step 1: Evaluate the range of reasonable notice by examining similar cases based on position, length of service, age, and circumstances. Establish a low, probable and high range.

Step 2: Establish the salary, wages and other remuneration that the former employee likely would have received over the period of notice.

Step 3: Establish the benefits and the value of those benefits that the employee would have received. Alternatively, establish the cost of replacing

36

benefits or benefits claims which would have been made had benefits been continued.

Step 4: Advise the employee of the duty to mitigate by diligently searching for alternative employment. Assuming compliance, once new employment is obtained, subtract remuneration earned through alternative employment from overall damages. However, if the employee receives higher overall remuneration, calculate the damages to the date of commencement of the new job.

Step 5: Calculate probable judgment interest and party and party costs.

Step 6: In those exceptional cases, if applicable, calculate general, aggravated or punitive damages.

Note: The net recovery to employee will be after payment of withholding tax, employee's premiums, and benefit repayment, if any, under the *E.I.A.*, and legal fees incurred to recover the additional severance.

2.7.1   REASONABLE NOTICE

o Notice of dismissal must be specific, unequivocal, and clearly communicated to the employee if it is to be effective in law. The onus of proving that notice was given is on the employer. See: *Parish v. Alberta* (1987), 81 A.R. 306 (Q.B.).

o The employer may give the employee actual working notice of dismissal or compensation in lieu of notice. Damages are a substitute for adequate notice and must be calculated from the date of the actual notice of termination.

o Notice begins when the employee has received proper notice of termination and the date of termination has been provided. However, in some cases a warning by the employer of pending elimination of employee's job has been taken into consideration in determining the reasonable notice period.

o Where there is some uncertainty as to the date of dismiss-al, damages do not start to run until the date of effective notice, or where no effective notice is given, the date the employee is actually dismissed.

o The amount of reasonable notice is a question of fact to be decided with reference to each particular case, having regard to the character of employment, the length of ser-vice, age of the employee, and the availability of similar employment, considering to the experience, training and qualifications of the employee. See: Appendix 2H – Rea-sonable Notice Periods – Alberta Cases.

o Where an employee is enticed or lured away from a former employer, he or she should be entitled to a longer period of notice. However, the inducement must go beyond the or-dinary degree of persuasion, and an employee who will-ingly leaves a secure job in order to pursue a new oppor-tunity has not necessarily been enticed.

o Where employment has been interrupted, the length of ser-vice will run from the re-hiring and not continuously through the interruption. However, this will not apply where there is an understanding to recognize past service by the employ-ee.

o Where there has been a transfer or sale of the business during employment, whether by shares or assets, service is usually regarded as continuous and total service is taken into account.

o Where it is customary in an industry to terminate employ-ment on a relatively short period of notice, courts may deem that the parties were aware of this customary stan-dard and, therefore, award a shorter period of notice.

o Generally, older employees (particularly those over 50) are entitled to a longer period of notice.

2.7.2   HEADS OF DAMAGES

(a)   General

o The purpose of damages in a wrongful dismissal action is to compensate the employee for loss of salary and other compensation, and loss of benefits over the period of reasonable notice.

o The amount of damages awarded is dependent on the amount of income which the employee would have earned during the period of reasonable notice. This is subject to a deduction in respect of any amount that the plaintiff earned or should have reasonably attained through alternative employment. The award is based on the actual loss of income from the former position and not the loss of earning capacity.

o In addition to the loss of salary that an employee would have earned during a period of notice, damages may be awarded to compensate for loss of non-discretionary bonuses, stock options, club dues, pension, insurance, medical plans, moving expenses, vacation pay, and other benefits which the employee could reasonably have expected had employment continued through the period of notice.

o An employee is entitled to any non-discretionary salary increase that would have been received had the employee not been terminated (e.g., a regular annual increase). However, where the increase is totally discretionary, courts will assume that it is very unlikely that the employee would have received the increase.

o Pre-judgment interest is awarded from the date of dismissal to the date of judgment.

(b) Fringe Benefits

- o Two general approaches are followed with respect to fringe benefits:
  - o One is to base the award on the cost of the company contribution to benefits. See: *Rahmath v. Louisiana Land & Exploration Co.* (1989), 59 D.L.R. (4th) 606 (Alta. C.A.).
  - o The other approach is to cover the actual costs that the employee incurs in replacing benefits, or damages based on benefits claims that the employee would have had (e.g., dental, unpaid health expenses, disability benefits, and, in the case of death during the reasonable notice period, the life insurance benefit). See: *Card Estate v. John A. Robertson Mechanical Contractors* (1989), 26 C.C.E.L. 294 (Ont. H.C.).

(c) Bonus

- o Discretionary bonuses are generally regarded as voluntary payments and therefore are not compensable in damages. Non-discretionary bonuses which are reasonably anticipated by the employee are properly included in damages.

(d) Pension Benefits

- o Damages for loss of pension benefits may be based on the loss of the employer's contributions to the pension plan over the appropriate notice period. Alternatively, the damages could be awarded for lost pension based on the capital value of the additional pension benefits that would have accrued during the period of reasonable notice. See: *Kowton v. Edmonton (City)* (1985), 38 Alta. L.R. (2d) 397 (Q.B.); *Boylan v. Canadian Broadcasting Corp.* (1994), 3 C.C.E.L. (2d) 64 (Alta. Q.B.).

- o If the pension would have vested during the reasonable notice period, the plaintiff is entitled to recover damages equivalent to the benefit of the vesting privilege.

(e) Holidays and Vacation Pay

o Damages may include accumulated vacation pay entitlement prior to the date of dismissal based on company policy or statutory vacation pay requirements. It also includes vacation pay that would have accrued during the period of reasonable notice.

o Where it is against company policy, a court will not award damages for an employee who claims for accumulated vacation pay.

(f) Other Special Damages Awarded

o Other special damages awarded include:
  o Expenses incurred in starting your own business, if incurred within the notice period.
  o Treatment costs for severe depression.
  o Compensation for loss of bargaining unit position.
  o Loss of investment income on collapse of an R.R.S.P.
  o Interest paid on a personal loan needed to cover personal expenses while between jobs.
  o Director's fees.
  o Reimbursement for repairs to company residence.
  o Compensation for living expenses during unemployment.

(g) Moving Costs and Related Expenses

o Some cases have allowed the former employee to claim costs of searching for new employment and new accommodation, as well as moving expenses incurred in mitigation of damages. However, some courts in Alberta have denied reimbursement for moving costs on the ground that these would have been incurred even if reasonable notice had been given. As a general rule, damages will not be awarded for an employee's loss on resale of his or her home, except where it results following negligent misrepresentation of the job. See: *Klapperbein v. Kamco Music & Sound Systems Ltd.* (1986), 49 Alta. L.R. (2d) 376 (C.A.); *Zylawy v. Edmonton (City)* (1985), 8 C.C.E.L. 93 (Alta. Q.B.).

o Other reasonable costs incurred in searching for new employment are compensable in damages, including long distance phone calls, résumé preparation, postage, career counselling, expenses arising to attend out-of-town interviews, gas, parking, business lunches, and necessary professional fees.

(h)   Loss of Reputation

o Damages for loss of reputation are not recoverable. However, if the employee is discredited in public by the former employer, he or she may be entitled to damages for slander.

o Where an employer unjustly refuses to provide references, and therefore makes it difficult to find alternative employment, the employee may be entitled to additional damages.

(i)   Mental Distress

o Damages for mental distress are recoverable if the claim arises from the dismissal itself, and not from some conduct or circumstances which occurred prior to or after the dismissal. Mental distress must be a separate, actionable wrong apart from the dismissal. It must result from the manner of dismissal, rather than the fact of the dismissal itself, or from a wanton and reckless breach of the employment contract. See: *Vorvis v. Insurance Corporation of British Columbia* (1989), [1989] 4 W.W.R. 218 (S.C.C.).

o The following behaviour by an employer has resulted in an award of damages for mental distress:
  o Unsubstantiated allegations of dishonesty or incompetence.
  o Unfounded allegations of just cause, despite a lack of any evidence.
  o Unfair treatment, particularly in failing to give reasons for the termination.
  o Terminating the employment by telephone while the employee was sick in bed.

o Failure to provide job references.

o Abrupt and insensitive termination of employment.

(j) Loss of Disability and Other Insurance Benefits

o Where an employee has wrongfully been denied disability or other insurance benefits as a result of the wrongful dismissal, the employer may be liable in damages for the loss of these benefits.

2.7.3 AGGRAVATED AND PUNITIVE DAMAGES

o In exceptional cases, where an employer's conduct has been extremely harsh, vindictive, malicious and reprehensible, it may justify a punitive damages award. See: *Vorvis v. Insurance Corporation of British Columbia* (1989), [1989] 4 W.W.R. 218 (S.C.C.); *Ambler v. J. Gilmour Interiors Inc.* (1992), 6 Alta. L.R. (3d) 176 (Q.B.).

2.7.4 TREATMENT OF OTHER INCOME AND PAYMENTS

(a) Unemployment Benefits

o Severance pay received from an employer will eliminate the entitlement to unemployment insurance during the period of notice related to that severance pay. See: *Unemployment Insurance Regulations*, C.R.C. 1978, c. 1576 (as amended), ss. 172 and 173.

o Unemployment benefits are deducted from the damages award.

o Section 45 of the *E.I.A.*, stipulates that where an employee receives any benefit in respect of a period over which he or she received unemployment benefits, including damages for wrongful dismissal, whether by way of a labour arbitration award, court judgment or otherwise, they must repay the unemployment benefits received with respect to the applicable period.

○ Section 46 of the *E.I.A.* requires an employer to ascertain the amount of unemployment benefits that would be repayable under s. 45 of that Act, and to deduct the amount of the unemployment benefits overpayment from any award.

(b) Disability Benefits

○ The cases are divided as to whether sickness and disability benefits which are paid to a terminated employee will be deducted from damages in lieu of reasonable notice of dismissal. This may turn on whether the benefits are in the nature of insurance payments or wages. Although not consistent with the courts in some other jurisdictions, the Alberta Court of Appeal has deducted W.C.B. benefits from damages for wrongful dismissal (see: *Salmi v. Greyfriar Developments Ltd.* (1985), 36 Alta. L.R. (2d) 182 (C.A.)). The same reasoning was applied in the case of disability benefits (see: *McGarry v. Bosco Homes Edmonton* (1992), 42 C.C.E.L. 198 (Alta. Q.B.)).

(c) Other Income

○ Where the employee had been in receipt of other income prior to the termination of employment, and continues to earn the same amount following termination, that will not be deducted from the damages claim.

(d) Pension

○ As pension benefits are not in the nature of wages, pension income will not be deducted from damages for wrongful dismissal.

2.7.5 DUTY TO MITIGATE

○ An employee who is wrongfully dismissed is under a duty to mitigate his or her damages by taking all reasonable steps to secure comparable, alternative employment.

o The onus is on the employer to show not only a lack of sufficient effort by the former employee, but also the availability of similar employment.

o The former employee need only establish that he or she made reasonable efforts to secure comparable, alternative employment.

o Where there is a contractual notice period or severance payment agreed to between the parties in advance, principles of mitigation do not usually apply.

o If the employee has been dismissed due to economic conditions, or because of inability to handle the job, it may constitute a failure to mitigate for them to refuse a reasonable alternative offer, so long as there is no acrimony or improper behaviour by the employer and no loss of prestige, embarrassment or humiliation to the employee.

o Failure to mitigate may result in dismissal of the plaintiff's action where a comparable position was refused shortly after the termination of employment. In most cases the court will subtract an amount estimated to be what the plaintiff could have earned in mitigation from the damages.

2.7.6   NEW EMPLOYMENT

o Any moneys earned by way of mitigation through alternative employment during the notice period are deducted from the damages otherwise payable to the employee.

o When the trial of a wrongful dismissal action takes place before the notice period has expired, the court may deduct a contingency amount based on its assessment as to whether the employee might find another job before the end of the notice period.

(a) Starting a New Business

o Generally, an employee can only commence his or her own business after exhausting the possibilities of obtaining an alternative position. Where this is seen to be unreasonable, damages could be reduced due to failure to mitigate, or the courts will accept the commencement of one's own business as fulfillment of the duty to mitigate.

(b) Retraining

o Where retraining is reasonable in order to enter a field with a better job opportunity, this will not constitute failure to mitigate.

(c) Maternity Leave

o Where an employee is terminated prior to or during a maternity leave, the period of reasonable notice will be postponed until completion of the maternity.

2.8 RELATED CAUSES OF ACTION AND REMEDIES

2.8.1 MISREPRESENTATION AND WRONGFUL HIRING

o Where, upon hiring or during employment, the employer has made a negligent or fraudulent misrepresentation, the employee may be entitled to damages. This is apart from any claim for breach of contract or wrongful dismissal. In order to establish an actionable misrepresentation it requires the following:

(i) Negligent or fraudulent misrepresentation.

(ii) Reliance on the misrepresentation by the employee.

(iii) Resulting damages.

o See: *Queen v. Cognos Inc.* (1993), [1993] 1 S.C.R. 87.

2.8.2 HARASSMENT

o Harassment by a supervisor may be actionable where it amounts to intentional infliction of mental suffering (see: *Boothman v. R.*, (1993), 49 C.C.E.L. 109 (Fed. T.D.)). However, the common law does not recognize a tort of sexual harassment and unless there was an actionable assault, this must be pursued by a complaint to the Alberta Human Rights Commission.

2.8.3 DEFAMATION

o Where the employer makes public statements which through independent action are slanderous, the employee can recover damages flowing from the slander.

o It appears that an action in defamation against the former employer can be combined with a wrongful dismissal action. See: *Perkins v. Brandon University* (1984), 33 Man. R. (2d) 152 (Q.B.), affirmed (1985) [1985] 5 W.W.R. 740 (C.A.); but see: *Makkar v. Scarborough (City)* (1985), 48 C.P.C. 141 (Ont. H.C.).

2.8.4 INDUCING BREACH OF CONTRACT

o A third party who has wrongfully induced the employer to terminate employment without reasonable notice, or has otherwise influenced the employee to breach their contractual obligations, may be liable for inducing breach of contract or intentional interference with economic relations. See: *Tree Savers International v. Savoy* (1991), 81 Alta. L.R. (2d) 325 (Q.B.), varied (1992), 84 Alta. L.R. (2d) 384 (C.A.).

o This could include a supervisor who may be personally liable if he or she acted maliciously or vindictively. See: *Morgan v. Saskatchewan* (1985), 43 Sask. R. 129 (C.A.); *Heslop v. Cooper's Crane Rental Ltd.* (1994), 6 C.C.E.L. (2d) 252 (Ont. Gen. Div.).

2.8.5   EMPLOYMENT STANDARDS CLAIMS

(a)   Alberta Legislation

o Employment standards benefits which cannot be recovered by a contractual claim at common law, should be the subject of a complaint to the Employment Standards Branch (e.g., vacation pay or overtime where not in written contract). See: *Chodan v. Banff Voyager Inn Ltd.* (1987), 88 C.L.L.C., 14,044 (Alta. Q.B.); *Allen v. International Union, U.M.W.A.* (1987), 52 Alta L.R. (2d) 386 (Q.B.). However, all other claims should be included in the common law action.

o The employee who wishes to sue for wrongful dismissal must be careful *not* to pursue a claim for the minimum period of notice set out in the *E.S.C.*. If any amount is recovered it could mean that the common law action for wrongful dismissal (where larger periods of notice and damages are available) is *res judicata*. See: *Rasanen v. Rosemount Industries Ltd.* (1994), 1 C.C.E.L. (2d) 161 (Ont. C.A.), leave to appeal to S.C.C. refused (1994), 7 C.C.E.L. (2d) 40.

(b)   Federal Legislation

o Where the employee is employed in a federal work or undertaking, he or she is subject to federal jurisdiction. A former employee may be entitled to statutory remedies for wrongful dismissal. The employee must not be in a managerial position, must have been continuously employed for a minimum of 12 consecutive months with the employer, and must not be a member of a group of employees subject to a collective agreement. See: *Canada Labour Code* ("*C.L.C.*"), R.S.C. 1985, c. L-2, ss. 167(3) and 240.

o The complaint must be made within ninety (90) days of the dismissal. See: s. 240(2), (3).

o Where the matter cannot be resolved by Labour Canada, it is set down before an adjudicator paid by the Federal Government. Where the adjudicator determines that the dismissal was unjust, he or she has the power to order the employer to pay compensation, reinstate the employee or do any other thing that is equitable to require the employer to remedy or counteract any consequence of dismissal. See: *Banca Nazionale del Lavoro of Canada Ltd.* (1988), 22 C.C.E.L. 59 (Fed. C.A.).

2.8.6 HUMAN RIGHTS

o If the dismissal of the employee is a result of discrimination under one of the prohibited grounds, in addition to common law rights of wrongful dismissal, it may violate federal or provincial human rights legislation.

o Under Alberta legislation, an employer is prohibited from discriminating against an employee on any of the following grounds: race, religious beliefs, colour, gender, physical disability, mental disability, age, ancestry, place of origin, family status or source of income. See: *H.R.C.M.A.*, s. 7.

o It is a complete defence if the employer can establish that the conduct is "reasonable and justifiable" in the circumstances or there is a *bona fide* occupational requirement (see: *H.R.C.M.A.*, s. 7(3)). The employer may still have a duty to accommodate to the point of undue hardship however (see: *Central Alberta Dairy Pool v. Alberta (Human Rights Commission)* (1990), [1990] 2 S.C.R. 489).

o For those employers under federal jurisdiction, they are subject to the *Canadian Human Rights Act*, R.S.C. 1985, c. H-6. That legislation prohibits discrimination on the following grounds: race, national or ethnic origin, colour, religion, age, sex, sexual orientation, marital status, family status, disability or conviction for offence for which a pardon has been granted. See: s. 2, as amended.

o Again, if the employer can establish a *bona fide* occupational requirement, it is a complete defence. See: *Canadian Human Rights Act*, s. 15.

o Any remedy under the human rights legislation is completely independent of common law rights and the human rights complaint may be filed and dealt with concurrently with the common law action for wrongful dismissal.

2.8.7   LABOUR BOARD

o In some cases, a dismissal of an employee may also give rise to various remedies under the labour relations legislation.

(a)   Unfair Labour Practices

o Where an employee is dismissed because of union activity or support for a trade union, then it constitutes an unfair labour practice contrary to the Alberta *Labour Relations Code*, S.A. 1988, c. L-1.2, or the *Canada Labour Code*, R.S.C. 1985, c. L-2, as applicable.

o Therefore, an employee who has been dismissed contrary to the labour relations legislation may seek reinstatement and other remedies in an application to the provincial or federal labour board.

(b)   Unsafe Work

o Employees have a right to refuse unsafe work. If an employee is dismissed after refusing to carry out unsafe work, he or she may seek reinstatement and other remedies under the provincial *Occupational Health and Safety Act*, R.S.A. 1980, c. O-2, s. 28.1.

o Under the *Canada Labour Code,* which applies to employees under federal jurisdiction, similar remedies are available. See: *C.L.C.*, ss. 128-132

2.9 OTHER EMPLOYEE CONSIDERATIONS

o Employees often have to consider other entitlements and benefits independently of the wrongful dismissal claim. These may include unemployment benefits, pension, life insurance, disability insurance and worker's compensation benefits.

2.9.1 UNEMPLOYMENT BENEFITS

o Most unemployed individuals who are eligible for unemployment benefits will need to file a claim, particularly those whose income is near or below the unemployment benefit maximum.

o The employer is obligated to issue a Record of Employment ("R.O.E."), which sets out the information required by the Canada Employment and Immigration Commission (the "commission") to establish the claim and entitlement. It also indicates the reason for issuing an R.O.E. Where the former employee disputes the reason indicated by the employer, he or she will be obligated to explain this to the commission officer.

o Although the R.O.E. (and other commission documents and information) is not compellable evidence for any purpose outside of the unemployment benefits scheme, it is prudent to check the R.O.E. Often the reason indicated by the employer on the R.O.E. is inconsistent with reasons advanced for termination of employment for purposes of defending a wrongful dismissal action. This can be a fruitful area for cross-examination.

o Individuals who lose their employment through wilful misconduct, or who freely resign or quit, are not eligible for unemployment benefits.

o When the reasons for termination of employment are disputed, the employee may be required to appeal the decision of the commission to a board of referees or an umpire.

However, even where an employee has lost his or her job for reasons which amount to just cause at common law, it is very difficult to establish wilful misconduct.

o Also, where the employee was compelled to resign or quit because of working conditions or other valid reasons, he or she will not be disqualified. For that reason, most employees are able to establish their entitlement to unemployment benefits.

o If an employee receives severance pay, this will eliminate entitlement to unemployment insurance during the period of notice related to that severance pay. See: *Unemployment Insurance Regulations, supra,* ss. 172 and 173.

o As mentioned, s. 45 of the *E.I.A.* stipulates that where an employee receives any benefit in respect of the period over which he or she received earnings or entitlements, including damages for wrongful dismissal, whether by way of a labour arbitration award, court judgment or otherwise, then they must repay the unemployment benefits received with respect to the applicable period.

o Section 46 of the *E.I.A.* requires an employer to ascertain the amount of unemployment benefits that would be repayable under s. 45 of the Act, and to deduct the amount of the overpayment (which was triggered by the labour arbitration award, court judgment or other remuneration, where an employer is required to pay earnings, including damages for wrongful dismissal to an employee). See: *Aliment Nationale L.B. Ltée v. Canadian Employment & Immigration Commission* (1990), 31 C.C.E.L. 187 (Fed. T.D.).

o Because of the obligation to repay benefits, if the employee obtains alternative employment prior to exhausting unemployment benefits and his or her salary was at or near the insurable maximum, the net recovery through wrongful dismissal litigation may be minimal. A large portion of the amount recovered simply goes to repay benefits. However, if the employee has exhausted his or her benefits, the repayment will entitle him or her to claim further unemployment benefits.

2.9.2   PENSION

o An employee who has been wrongfully dismissed may be eligible for early retirement or full pension.

o Moneys received through pension are not deductible from the damages that the employee is entitled to for wrongful dismissal.

2.9.3   LIFE INSURANCE

o Where an employee was entitled to group life insurance during employment, he or she usually has a right to convert the life insurance to an individual policy within a stipulated period of time following termination of employment. In most cases the employee is not obligated to have a qualifying medical. However, the premiums will be much higher than that paid under the group life insurance plan.

Note: In the case of a wrongful dismissal, where an employer has prematurely terminated the life insurance coverage prior to the end of the period of reasonable notice, and the employee has not accepted compensation for loss of benefits and released the employer of any further liability, the employer may be exposed to a life insurance claim. In Card Estate v. John A. Robertson Mechanical Contractors (1985) Ltd. (1989), 26 C.C.E.L. 294 (Ont. H.C.), the employer forced an ill employee to take three months unpaid leave. There was no guarantee of work available after the leave. The court held that the employee had been constructively dismissed. The employer failed to tell the employee upon termination from the group life insurance that he had 31 days to convert to individual coverage. The deceased employee's wife was awarded damages against the employer for life insurance proceeds that she would have received but for the wrongful dismissal.

2.9.4   DISABILITY INSURANCE

o A disabled employee may also be entitled to disability benefits either directly from the employer or through a group disability insurance policy.

o The law is uncertain as to whether disability insurance benefits are deductible from damages for wrongful dismissal. See: D'Andrea, Corry and Forester, *Illness and Disability in the Workplace*, (Canada Law Book, 1996), para. 2:5000.

o Many employers will terminate disability coverage effective the date of termination of employment. Where an employee has been wrongfully denied disability or other insurance benefits as a result of a wrongful dismissal, an employer may be liable in damages for loss of disability benefits. See: *Tarailo v. Allied Chemical Canada Ltd.* (1989), 68 O.R. (2d) 288 (H.C.), appeal settled on consent of all parties (1992), 7 O.R. (3d) 318 (C.A.); *George v. Morden & Helwig Ltd.* (1988), 20 C.C.E.L. 29 (Ont. H.C.); *Casey v. General Inc.* (1988), 24 C.C.E.L. 142 (Nfld. T.D.).

2.9.5   WORKER'S COMPENSATION

o An employee who has been dismissed following a work-related injury or industrial accident will be entitled to claim worker's compensation benefits.

o Although the courts in some jurisdictions have held that W.C.B. benefits are not deductible from damages for wrongful dismissal, the current law in Alberta states that they are. See: *Salmi v. Greyfriar Developments Ltd.* (1983), 27 Alta. L.R. (2d) 204 (Q.B.), reversed (1985), 36 Alta. L.R. (2d) 182 (C.A.); but see: *McKay v. Camco Inc.* (1986), 11 C.C.E.L. 256 (Ont. C.A.).

o Dismissal from employment will not detrimentally affect W.C.B. entitlement. The key to coverage is to establish that the illness or disability is related to an industrial accident.

2.10 TACTICAL CONSIDERATIONS AND STRATEGIES

o The most important objective when acting on behalf of a plaintiff in a wrongful dismissal action is to obtain the maximum severance package in the shortest period of time, while minimizing legal expenses. Given the competing interests of the employee and the employer, this is easier said than done. However, the following are some strategies to consider:

  o If the former employee's relationship is cordial with a key member of the employer's management, suggest that the employee arrange a meeting to discuss settlement. Help your client prepare for the meeting by explaining his legal rights, including mediation. Consider providing a table of relevant cases that can be reviewed at the meeting. Monitor the progress and encourage the client to call you if he or she has any questions.

  o If the client is successful in direct negotiations, ensure that the settlement is structured in a way that meets the client's needs and minimizes the tax impact. Ensure that all closing documentation is reviewed prior to signature.

  o If direct negotiations are not successful, or are not practicable under the circumstances, draft a demand letter as quickly as possible to be delivered to senior management. The letter should be brought to the attention of a member of the management team who has the requisite authority to settle the matter. The demand letter should provide for a maximum of seven days to resolve the matter, failing which you will recommend that the matter proceed to litigation.

  o If sufficient progress in the settlement negotiations has not been made within the seven days, draft, file, and serve the statement of claim as quickly as possible.

  o Move the action along to the next steps as quickly as possible. Entertain settlement negotiations at every opportunity.

  o Develop a working relationship with your staff and colleagues so that the action can progress as quickly as possible, even when you are absent or busy.

o Through regular communications with your client, inquire as to the success of the job search efforts. Ensure that the client contacts you as soon as possible after an offer of employment has been received. At that stage you will have to ascertain the impact that the job will have on potential damages and modify your client's negotiation position accordingly.

o In an appropriate case, where there are no serious facts or legal issues in dispute, consider a summary judgment application.

2.11 DEMAND LETTER

o The best time to draft the demand letter is immediately following the meeting with the client. The demand letter should be directed to a member of the senior management team who has the authority to negotiate and agree to a settlement.

o The demand letter should be brief, outline the key facts, advise the employer as to the potential range of damages, provide a table of cases as authority for that position, and make a specific demand for payment which is acceptable to the client.

o The demand letter should be reviewed with the client prior to it being sent to ensure that the facts and the amount requested are acceptable. To save time, this can be done by telephone or telefax. Alternatively, a meeting should be arranged to review the demand letter.

o Make sure the demand letter is "without prejudice." As the letter is a genuine attempt to resolve the dispute, it will not be admissible in further proceedings, and therefore cannot be used to your client's detriment at a later date if settlement has not been achieved. See Appendix 2B – Sample Demand Letter.

2.12 RETAINER AGREEMENT OR LETTER

o A retainer letter should be sent to the client, or a retainer agreement entered into.

o In order to comply with the *Code of Professional Conduct* of the Law Society of Alberta, the letter should:
  o Fully explain the litigation process and the time that it is expected to take.
  o Fully explain the nature of a wrongful dismissal action and a preliminary evaluation of the claim.
  o Give an explanation of the basis for calculating legal fees, billing for other charges and disbursements.
  o Fully explain the frequency of rendering accounts, the time for payment and interest charges.
  o Encourage the client to contact you if he or she has any concerns about the account with an offer to meet and resolve any concerns.
  o Emphasize that settlement depends on reaching an agreement which is acceptable to the former employer. If the matter is not settled the only option is to continue with the litigation which will take considerable time. The court can only award a judgment, and the collection of that judgment depends on either voluntary payment by the employer or execution proceedings. If the employer becomes insolvent or bankrupt in the meantime, then the judgment may only be an unsecured claim.

o The Law Society of Alberta has an excellent pamphlet on lawyers' legal fees and on the litigation process that may be included with the letter. These may be ordered through the Law Society.

o See Appendix 2C – Sample Retainer Letter, and Appendix 2D – Sample Retainer Agreement.

2.13 STATEMENT OF CLAIM

o The statement of claim should clearly and concisely set out the material facts for the wrongful dismissal action and any related claim. These include:

o The hiring, position, duties and term of employment.
o A plea that the plaintiff faithfully and diligently performed the job.
o Final salary, other compensation and benefits.
o Termination without reasonable notice or just cause.
o If applicable, the period of unemployment and details regarding alternative employment.
o A brief explanation and estimate of damages.
o Prayer for relief to include damages, judgment interest and costs.

o See Appendix 2G – Sample Statement of Claim.

2.14   ACTION

o Prepare a "to do" checklist at the conclusion of the client interview.

2.14.1   THE LAWYER'S "TO DO" CHECKLIST

o Consider placing the following on your "to do" list:
o Evaluate the period of reasonable notice, heads of damage and range of damages.
o Prepare a table of cases in support of the claim.
o Research any issues regarding cause.
o Review all relevant documents, including offer letter, employment contract, policies, benefit information, income tax returns, recent cheque stubs, evaluations, warning letters, letters of termination of employment, record of employment, letters of reference, client's résumé, etc.
o Where just cause is in issue, interview any witnesses, including former employers and supervisors. If they are co-operative, you may also want to talk to current employees.
o Draft demand letter, review with client and send to the employer.
o Contact other former employees to discuss whether settlement was reached, any details, whether resolved quickly or not, etc.

o Enter limitation date in diary system.

Note: <u>Common Limitation Dates</u>

<u>Action</u>	<u>Limitation Period</u>
Wrongful dismissal/breach of contract	6 years[1]
Related tort action	2 years[2]
Discrimination Contrary to Human Rights Legislation	1 year[3]

---

1. *Limitations of Actions Act*, R.S.A. 1980, c. L-15, s. 4(1)(c).

2. *Limitations of Actions Act*, s. 51; *E.S.C.*, s. 98: 1 year with option for additional year for unpaid wages, overtime pay, holiday pay, general holidays, etc.

3. *H.R.C.M.A.*, s. 19(2).

o Send retainer letter or agreement to client.
o Where applicable, follow up with the Human Rights Commission, Employment Standards, or Canada Employment and Immigration Commission regarding related matters.

2.14.2   THE CLIENT'S "TO DO" CHECK LIST

o Prepare a standard client "to do" checklist which includes a list of matters which the client will attend to. This list should include the following:

o Obtain copies of any documentation that has not already been provided including résumé, offer letter, employment contract, policies, benefits information, income tax returns, recent cheque stubs, evaluations, warning letters, letter of termination of employment, record of employment, letters of reference, client diaries and notes, etc.

o Write a detailed summary including details of hiring, summary of the employment situation, comments regarding evaluations and job performance, and details of all circumstances surrounding termination of employment.

- o Prepare a job search record consisting of résumé, clippings from newspaper job advertisements applied to, letters of application to employers, and a summary of all contact with the potential new employers including results of interviews.
- o Keep record/receipts of all expenses incurred in searching for alternative employment.
- o Advise as to status of unemployment benefit claim and keep all copies of relevant documents.
- o Advise as soon as new employment is offered.
- o Other Matters: _____

_____
_____
_____

APPENDIX 2A
Client Interview Checklist
Wrongful Dismissal Action, Former Employee

Referred by _____ Date of Interview _____

Date of Termination
Name _____ of Employment _____

Address _____

_____ Telephone: _____

_____ Telefax: _____

Age _____

Name of Spouse _____

Name of Former Employer _____

Address of Former Employer _____

Name/Title of Immediate Supervisor _____

Name/Title for Contact for Demand Letter/Negotiations _____

_____

Address, Telephone and Telefax number, if different from above _____

_____

Reporting Structure _____

_____

_____

_____

_____

_____

(use back if necessary)

Review résumé, employment and educational background _____

_____

_____

☐   Check if résumé attached.
☐   Client to prepare and provide résumé.

Hiring and Interview for Job with Former Employer

Advertisement or Posting   ❏   Yes   ❏   No

How found out about job?

Unemployed at time?

Who interviewed? Any representations made? Any issue as to fraudulent or negligent misrepresentations?   ❏   Yes   ❏   No

Details _____

_____

_____

_____

Letter of hire?   ❏   Yes   ❏   No

Sign any documents?   ❏   Yes   ❏   No

If yes, what documents? _____

_____

Employment Contract?   ❏   Yes   ❏   No

Confidentiality/Non-competition Agreement?

     ❏   Yes   ❏   No

Others?   ❏   Yes   ❏   No

Member of Union? Collective Agreement?

     ❏   Yes   ❏   No

Job History

Training provided?   ❏   Yes   ❏   No

Date/Details _____

_____

Probation period and results? _____

_____

Employment

Name of Employer _____

Dates: From _____ to _____, Years: ____

Title _____

Supervisor _____

Place _____

Salary _____

Job Performance

Details of Evaluation?

- Warnings?

- Discipline?

How well did you get along with other:

- Supervisors

- Colleagues

Circumstances Leading to Termination _____

_____

_____

_____

Reasons for Termination _____

_____

_____

_____

Is cause in issue?

❏   Yes   ❏   No

Damages Evaluation

Salary/Wages? _____

Any expected increases? _____

Other remuneration? _____

Bonuses?

     ❏ Discretionary   Details: _____

     ❏ Non-discretionary _____

Overtime (yearly/monthly/average) _____

Commissions? _____

Other _____

Incentive Plans?	❏	Yes	❏	No
Stock Options?	❏	Yes	❏	No
Savings Plan?	❏	Yes	❏	No

Stock Purchase Plan _____

_____

Others _____

_____

Retirement Plan

Pension	❏	Yes	❏	No
Group R.R.S.P.	❏	Yes	❏	No.
Other	❏	Yes	❏	No

Details _____

_____

Review all pension documents, statements, group R.R.S.P., etc.

                    ❏   Yes   ❏   No

Benefits

BENEFITS	YES	NO	EMPLOYEE	EMPLOYER
Short-term Illness/Disability				
Long-term Disability				
Life Insurance • Basic • Additional Amount _____ • Conversion Options ❏ Yes ❏ No _____ days				
Accidental Death & Dismemberment				
Alberta Health Care ❏ Family ❏ Single				
Extended Health				
Dental				

Automobile/Travel Benefits. Details _____

_____

Other Benefits _____

_____

Vacation – Annual Amount _____

Any accrued/unused vacation?   ❏ Yes   ❏ No

Amount _____

Vacation Pay Received?   ❏ Yes   ❏ No

Disability/Worker's Compensation

W.C.B.?   ❏ Yes   ❏ No

On L.T.D.?   ❏ Yes   ❏ No

Details of carrier and status of claim _____

_____

Applied for unemployment benefits? ❏ Yes ❏ No

Record of Employment issued? ❏ Yes ❏ No

Reviewed any issue as to entitlement? ❏ Yes ❏ No

Details _____

_____

Pension/Retirement Issues

Are there any pension or retirement issues? ❏ Yes ❏ No

Expected age of retirement _____

How long? _____

Pension vested? _____

Type of pension?

❏ Define benefit

❏ Define contribution

❏ Other

Options?

❏ Leave in plan

❏ Transfer to other pension

❏ Transfer to R.R.S.P.

Has client received pension advice? ❏ Yes ❏ No

Advisor _____

Final Paycheque

All wages, salary and other remuneration
paid to date? ❏ Yes ❏ No

Vacation pay? ❏ Yes ❏ No

Any pay in lieu of notice?	❑ Yes	❑ No
Letters of reference provided?	❑ Yes	❑ No
Has the client asked for any?	❑ Yes	❑ No

Related Actions

Employment Standards claim?   ❑ Yes   ❑ No

Details:

_____

Human Rights claim?   ❑ Yes   ❑ No

Details:

_____

Severance package offered?   ❑ Yes   ❑ No

Reviewed   ❑

Details:

_____

Settlement discussions?   ❑ Yes   ❑ No

Details:

_____

Outplacement counselling?   ❑ Yes   ❑ No

Name of outplacement counsellor _____

Client's future plans? _____

_____

_____

Job search and expectations regarding new employment? _____

_____

_____

APPENDIX 2B
Sample Demand Letter

Lawyer's Name
Direct Line: (403) 250-0000
Our File No.: *

* Date

* Address

Dear *:

Re: *
*

We act on behalf of * in the matter of his dismissal from *. We are of the view that the severance package offered to * is inadequate under the circumstances, and are writing to outline our client's position, and hopefully to resolve our client's claim without resorting to litigation.

Our client has spent the majority of his working career with *, having been employed there for * years. At the time of the termination of his employment he was the *. Prior to that, *. Throughout his employment with *, we understand that our client was a dedicated and concientious employee. He was terminated from his employment on * because *. At the time of the termination of employment he was earning $* per month. In addition he received certain company benefits.

At the time that our client's employment was terminated, you provided * weeks' pay in lieu of reasonable notice of dismissal pursuant to the *Employment Standards Code*. You also offered a small severance package consisting of a lump sum of * months' pay and bridging payments for up to * months.

We are of the view that our client is entitled to compensation for * months' salary and loss of benefits in lieu of reasonable notice of dismissal pursuant to the common law. We have relied upon those cases which are attached in support of our conclusion in this regard. We calculate * months' salary as $*. In addition, we estimate that the value of our client's benefits is 10% of his overall salary. We therefore demand that the lump sum severance package to be paid to our client in lieu of reasonable notice of dismissal be $*.

Our client's offer is open for acceptance until the close of business on *, failing which it will be automatically withdrawn.

If you are prepared to accept this offer, we request the opportunity to allocate the severance amount toward reasonable solicitor and client fees and a retiring allowance. In addition, we request the opportunity to file a duly executed Revenue Canada TD-2 form in order to roll all or a portion of the severance amount into our client's R.R.S.P.

We look forward to your reply. In the event that this matter has not been amiably resolved by *, we will recommend that our client commence litigation.

Yours truly,

LAW FIRM NAME

Lawyer's Name

cc *

APPENDIX 2C
Sample Retainer Letter

Lawyer's Name
Direct Line: (403) 250-0000
Our File No.: 11111-1

* Date

* Address

Dear Sir:

Re: *

We wish to thank you for retaining our firm to act on your behalf in regard to the above action. We are writing to confirm that we are prepared to act on your behalf and to outline the terms of our understanding.

Following our initial consultation on *, you instructed us to prepare a demand letter for your former employer regarding your wrongful dismissal, and to outline the amount of compensation that would be acceptable to you in lieu of reasonable notice of termination. A copy of the demand letter is enclosed for your information and records. If a reasonable settlement offer has not been agreed to by the expiry date set out in that letter, then you have instructed us to issue a Statement of Claim against your former employer commencing litigation in the Alberta Court of Queen's Bench. Once the Statement of Claim has been served on your former employer, your employer will be required to file a Statement of Defence, and usually will retain counsel to defend against your claim. The Court allows 15 days from the date of service of the Statement of Claim for your employer to prepare and file a Statement of Defence. However, this deadline is commonly extended as a courtesy as between counsel to enable your employer sufficient time to retain a lawyer and to prepare a Statement of Defence. If you do not wish us to grant any extension to the opposite party in this action, please advise us immediately so that we can make your position clear to the other party.

Once all of the pleadings have been filed and closed, then Examinations for Discovery will be held whereby we will be given an opportunity to examine an officer of your former employer and their counsel will be given an opportunity to examine you. Upon completion of the Examinations for Discovery and all other interlocutory matters, the action will then be set down for trial.

It is anticipated that most of the work with respect to this litigation will be performed by the writer, however, other lawyers in our firm may be utilized to perform legal services where, in our judgment, such assistance is necessary or desirable, particularly where a more junior lawyer can perform services in a more cost-effective manner.

Our fees will be based principally on the time spent by us on your behalf, although we reserve the right to adjust our rates in appropriate circumstances, such as where exceptionally efficient representation is made, or where circumstances are pressing or where special demands may be made of us. We also confirm that the writer's current hourly rate is $240.00 per hour, which is subject to be increased from time to time, and is reviewed on an annual basis in May. We also advise that the amount charged per hour increases with the experience and seniority of the lawyer conducting work on your behalf and if more senior counsel are involved, the hourly rate can be higher than that of the writer.

You will also be responsible for reimbursing us for disbursements and other charges incurred on your behalf. Such disbursements and other charges may include expenses such as telephone calls, postage, deliveries, photocopying, telecopies, court fees, word processing, and other reasonable out-of-pocket expenses.

At this stage, we cannot accurately assess what our legal fees might be, and this is particularly difficult when you are involved in litigation. Although the majority of cases settle prior to trial, the acceptance or rejection of a settlement depends ultimately on whether your former employer offers a settlement which is acceptable to you. If a reasonable settlement is not offered, then your only alternative is to proceed with the litigation and ultimately to trial against your former employer. The amount of the total legal fees involved will depend largely on the steps taken in this action.

We shall require an initial retainer of $*, which will serve as a source of payment of our interim accounts when rendered. We also confirm that you will be providing us with a series of post-dated cheques in the amount of $* to be deposited each month as a retainer toward future legal fees. Any unused portion of the retainer will be returned to you upon completion of our services, and as the retainer is used from time to time a further retainer may be requested.

Interim accounts will be rendered on a regular basis, and will detail the services performed, the legal fees charged, and the disbursements incurred. A final account will be rendered at the conclusion of the action, taking into consideration a number of factors. If you have any questions concerning our accounts, please feel free to discuss it with us. If you feel that the fee charged is unfair, you have a right to have the account taxed before a Taxing Officer of the Court of Queen's Bench. In regard to lawyer's fees, you may wish to refer to the enclosed brochure which is published by the Law Society of Alberta.

Accounts must be paid within 15 days of receipt. If any account remains overdue, the firm has the right to cease all further work until full payment has been made, and may cease to act on your behalf should that be necessary. In addition, legal proceedings may be taken in order to collect the outstanding account.

As we advised you during our initial meeting on *, in our view, dismissal due to economic circumstances, or corporate reorganization does not constitute just cause at Common Law. Furthermore, while the severance pay offered to you in the sum of $* constitutes an appropriate amount under the *Employment Standards Code* of Alberta, you would be entitled to a longer period of notice or pay in lieu of notice under the Common Law.

However, in considering whether to engage in litigation against your former employer, and to assess the benefits of any severance package which is offered, you should consider the following:

> 1. If you subsequently agree to a severance package which is acceptable to you, or if you recover a judgment against your former employer following a trial, the damages in lieu of reasonable notice of dismissal will constitute a "retiring allowance" and you will be required to repay the unemployment benefits which have been calculated over the same period as the retiring allowance. While your unemployment entitlement would be deferred, if you have been able to secure employment before your unemployment benefits run out, then you will be required to repay the unemployment benefits but will not receive any additional unemployment entitlement because you had been able to commence work before the unemployment benefits ran out.

> 2. A severance package which has been agreed to, or a Court judgment for wrongful dismissal is subject to a withholding tax. The only way to avoid the payment of withholding tax is to roll over all or a portion of your severance package to an R.R.S.P. This is subject to certain limits stipulated by Revenue Canada pursuant to the *Income Tax Act* and the regulations under the *Income Tax Act*. You may wish to contact Revenue Canada for further information in this regard, or contact your tax advisor.

> 3. You are under a duty to seek alternative employment as diligently as possible. If you are not actively seeking alternative employment, your damages award could ultimately be reduced for "failure to mitigate your damages". Furthermore, once you obtain alternative employment, the amount that you earn in your new job may reduce the damages award to which you are otherwise entitled at Common Law. For this reason, we have advised you to actively seek work and to keep an accurate record of your job search.

4. Until a severance package has been agreed to with your former employer, or until a Court judgment has actually been paid by your former employer, you are not entitled to claim your legal fees as a tax deduction. If you later recover money, then the legal fees are deductible against the tax paid on the "retiring allowance".

As we advised during our initial consultation, the above factors often make wrongful dismissal litigation uneconomical unless a reasonable settlement can be negotiated very early in the litigation process. We appreciate that you have carefully weighed the advantages and disadvantages of pursuing your former employer in Court and that your instructions at this time are to proceed with a demand letter followed by issuance of a Statement of Claim commencing litigation against your former employer for wrongful dismissal.

We are appreciative of this opportunity to be of service. Should you have any questions or concerns regarding these arrangements, the service provided by us, or our advice to date, we would be pleased to discuss this with you.

Yours very truly,

LAW FIRM NAME

Lawyer's Name

APPENDIX 2D
Sample Retainer Agreement

RETAINER AGREEMENT (NO CONTINGENCY)

THIS RETAINER AGREEMENT made this ____ day of _____, 19__,

BETWEEN:

[CLIENT]
(hereinafter referred to as "the client")

OF THE FIRST PART

- and -

LAW FIRM NAME
(hereinafter referred to as "the solicitors")

OF THE SECOND PART

WHEREAS:

1. The client wishes to retain the services of the solicitors and to have the solicitors act on his behalf in accordance with the terms and conditions hereinafter set forth.

NOW THEREFORE IN CONSIDERATION OF THE COVENANTS HEREIN CONTAINED THE CLIENT AND THE SOLICITORS AGREE AS FOLLOWS:

1. The client does hereby retain and employ the solicitor as barristers and solicitors.

2. The solicitors hereby accept such retainer and employment on account of the matters for which they have been retained by the client; namely, *

and shall, in the performance of such services, use their best skill and ability and in good faith and in every way advance and protect the rights of the client in such matters insofar as this may be done in accordance with law and the ethical standards of the legal profession.

3. The client agrees that the solicitors may, in the performance of the services to be rendered on behalf of the client, retain such persons, corporations or firms as the solicitors shall deem necessary to the advancement of the client's interest.

4. It is understood and agreed that the solicitors shall have full authority in the handling and conduct of all negotiations as may be required but shall not settle or compromise the legal position of the client without first obtaining the consent of the client and the solicitors and shall be entitled to take any steps which may be necessary or proper, in the solicitors opinion, to protect the interest of the client.

5.   (a) The client shall have the right, at any time, with or without reason, to terminate and end the retainer and the employment of the solicitors and to obtain a new attorney or to take such steps as he deems proper.

(b) It is understood by and between the parties hereto that the solicitors may hereafter deem it necessary or advisable for personal or other reasons to withdraw as solicitors for the client. In such event the solicitors shall have the full right and authority to so withdraw. For such purposes the solicitor shall notify the client in writing and for a reasonable time thereafter but for not more than fifteen (15) days thereafter the solicitors shall take all steps reasonable and necessary to protect the interest of the client until the client has had a reasonable opportunity to obtain new representation should he so desire.

6.   (a) The solicitors shall be entitled to be paid for all expenses actually paid or necessarily incurred on behalf of the client; such expenses being hereinafter termed "disbursements".

(b) The solicitors shall be entitled to be paid for the professional services rendered for and on behalf of the client. The fees to which the solicitor shall be entitled shall be dependant upon the complexity of the matters under consideration, the urgency of the matters under consideration and the results obtained for the client; PROVIDED, HOW-EVER, that the solicitors shall be entitled to a minimum remuneration equal to the product derived by multiplying the number of hours charged to the client's file by the hourly billing rates (as determined from time to time by the solicitors' Management Committee) of the various lawyers engaged in providing services to the client.

(c) The client shall be responsible for any Goods and Services Tax that may be payable upon the fee and any disbursements in respect of the cause of action and shall pay this amount to the solicitors.

(d) The client hereby deposits with the solicitor the sum of $* which shall be retained by the solicitors in the solicitors' trust account as security for application on the ultimate balance owing for fees and disbursements from the client to the solicitors.

(e) The client agrees that in the event the solicitors are in receipt of any monies for or on behalf of the client, howsoever arising, the solicitors shall be secured in respect thereof and shall have a first and paramount lien thereon for fees and disbursements properly due the solicitors and the client irrevocably authorizes and directs the said solicitors to deduct the amount of their proper fees and disbursements from any monies coming into the solicitors' possession.

(f) At the request of the client the solicitors agree to render interim accounts on a regular basis and the client agrees that he will pay such accounts upon receipt, failing which the client agrees to pay interest at the rate of *% *per annum* on any outstanding accounts from 30 days following the date thereof until the date of payment.

(g) At the request of the client at any time and from time to time, the solicitors agree to account to the client for all monies received for and on behalf of the client and to pay such monies which are owing to the client.

(h) The client acknowledges that he has been advised by the solicitors that in the event he has a complaint about the services performed by the solicitors or the fees charged therefor, that such a complaint may be advanced with the Law Society of Alberta; and, in respect of fees, the client may have same taxed by the Court of Queen's Bench of Alberta. In respect of a disagreement as to the amount of fees, the parties submit to the jurisdiction of the Court of Queen's Bench, Judicial Centre of *, and agree to be bound by the decision of the Courts of the Province of Alberta and do attorn to the jurisdiction of the said Courts for such purposes.

7. In the event that the solicitors perform additional work for the client on matters other than those particularized in paragraph 2 hereof, the parties agree that the provisions of this agreement shall prevail it being the parties' intention that all professional services provided by the solicitors to or on behalf of the client now or in the future will be governed by the terms herein.

8. With the exception of those documents lent by the client to the solicitors, all documents which came into the possession of the solicitors or which are created by the solicitors on the client's behalf, shall be the property of the solicitors. The client is entitled to obtain any copies of the documents upon payment of the cost of photocopying. The solicitors are entitled to retain a lien over any documents, including photocopies, belonging to the client which are in the possession of the solicitors, pending payment of any outstanding accounts which the client owes to the solicitors.

9. This agreement shall not be assignable by either party.

10. This agreement shall be binding upon the parties hereto, their heirs, executors and administrators.

      IN WITNESS WHEREOF the client and the solicitors have hereunto affixed their hands and seals as of the date and year first above written.

_____	)	_____
Witness	)	[Client]
	)	
	)	
	)	
	)	LAW FIRM NAME
	)	
_____	)	
Witness	)	Per: _____
	)	Partner
	)	
_____	)	
Witness	)	Per: _____
	)	Partner

APPENDIX 2E
Lawyer's Checklist

(To be completed upon opening file)

1. Name of Client:

2. Name of Employer:

3. Date of Dismissal:

4. Notice Given:

5. Amount of Severance paid:

6. Issue as to cause:

7. Range of reasonable notice:

8. Range of damages:

9. Responsible lawyer:

10. Assisting lawyer:

11. Clerk responsible:

12. Limitation periods?

ACTION	FILE STATEMENT OF CLAIM BY
Wrongful Dismissal	_____
Breach of Contract	_____
Tort or Related Action	_____

	FILE CLAIM BY
Employment Standards	_____
Human Rights	_____

13. Timelines for Initial Steps:

Send demand letter by: _____

Time to respond to demand letter: _____

Deadline for filing and service
of statement of claim: _____

Other special considerations? _____

APPENDIX 2F
Litigation Checklist – Employee

1.   **ARE WE FREE TO ACT?**

_____ Do we act for the proposed opposite parties? (If the opposite party is a corporation, do we act for directors, shareholders or related corporation?)

_____ Is there any possibility that any of our regular clients will be brought into the action by way of third party proceedings or otherwise?

_____ Are any of the lawyers at the firm a director or shareholder of the opposite party or of a related corporation?

2.   **CLIENT**

_____ Advised of fee basis?

_____ Advised of economics of wrongful dismissal litigation?

_____ Extent of your authority defined?

_____ Advised of possible length of litigation?

_____ Advised that you cannot guarantee success?

_____ Terms of retainer confirmed in writing?

If corporate client, consider obtaining directors resolution confirming:
_____ Conditions of retainer
_____ From whom instruction may be taken
_____ To whom reports may be made

_____ Has likelihood of successful collection of judgment been canvassed with client?

NOTE: Client should be kept informed of each step as matter progresses. All instructions should be confirmed in writing.

3.   **LIMITATION DATES**

_____ Enter in Limitations Diary

_____ Enter in own diary

_____ Note date on face of file

_____ As each date is met, enter new limitation date

_____ Treat Rule 11 as limitation date for service of Statement of Claim

4. **ARE THERE CONDITIONS PRECEDENT TO ACTION?**

_____ Time limits on giving notice if one is suing municipal or government bodies;

_____ Contractual conditions precedent such as demand or proof of loss or exhausting remedies;

_____ Consent to sue needed?

5. **JURISDICTION**

_____ Is action properly brought in Alberta? Can all defendants be served here?

_____ Any chance Federal Court involved?

_____ Exclusive jurisdiction in other body like Workers' Compensation Board or Public Utilities Board?

_____ Should action be brought elsewhere for any reason? (e.g., higher damage awards in another jurisdiction, for purposes of collection, etc.)

6. **CAPACITY**

_____ (e.g., infant, mental incompetent, estate, partnership?)

7. **CRIMINAL OR OTHER PROCEEDINGS OR HEARINGS**

_____ Have there been any?

8. **WORKERS' COMPENSATION ACT**

_____ Are any claimants covered?

_____ Has consent been obtained?

9. **COMPULSORY JOINDER**

_____ Are there any joint parties?

10. **HAVE PARTIES BEEN PROPERLY IDENTIFIED?**

_____ Proper corporate name?

80

_____ Limited liability – any arguments against?

_____ Partnership (join all parties)?

_____ Agency?

_____ Guarantees?

_____ Representative of estate deceased?

11. **REVIEW   ALL   RELEVANT   STATUTES   AND REGULATIONS**

List below all prevalent statutes and regulations

_____ All limitation periods noted and diarized

_____

_____

_____

_____

_____

APPENDIX 2G
Sample Statement of Claim

IN THE COURT OF QUEEN'S BENCH OF ALBERTA
JUDICIAL CENTRE OF *

BETWEEN:

*

Plaintiff

- and -

*

Defendant

STATEMENT OF CLAIM
(sample)

1. The Plaintiff resides in the City of [**Place**], in the Province of Alberta.

2. The Defendant is incorporated as a Hospital District under the laws of Alberta pursuant to the *Hospitals Act*, R.S.A. 1980, c. H-11, and operates a number of auxiliary hospitals and nursing homes in the City of [**Name**].

(The Defendant is extra-provincially registered under the laws of Alberta, and carries on business in Alberta with offices in the City of Calgary.)

3. The Plaintiff commenced employment with the Defendant on or about [**date**] as a Dietary Aide, at the [**Name**] Hospital in [**Place**], Alberta. After approximately 8 months she was promoted to the position of Food Services Supervisor at the [**Name**] Hospital in [**Place**], Alberta.

4. The Plaintiff faithfully and diligently performed her duties on behalf of the Defendant, and throughout her employment with the Defendant the Plaintiff proved herself to be a valuable and reliable employee.

5. On or about [**date**], the Plaintiff was dismissed from the Defendant's employ without just cause and without any notice.

6. The Plaintiff was receiving an annual salary of $[**amount**] at the date of her dismissal.

7. The Plaintiff was also entitled, as of the date of dismissal, to certain benefits, including:

　　(a) Alberta Health Care;

(b) Drug and Medical Plan coverage;

(c) Dental Plan coverage;

(d) Short term and long term disability;

(e) Basic and optional life insurance;

(f) Basic, optional and voluntary Accidental Death and Dismemberment Insurance;

(g) Pension Plan coverage.

The Defendant made annual contributions on behalf of the Plaintiff for the above benefits in the amount of $[**amount**].

8. The Plaintiff has incurred numerous and various out-of-pocket expenses due to the Defendant's wrongful termination of her employment in her attempts to mitigate her damage in seeking alternative employment.

9. The Plaintiff proposes that the trial of this action be held in the City of Calgary, in the Province of Alberta.

WHEREFORE THE PLAINTIFF CLAIMS:

(a) Damages for wrongful dismissal in the sum of $70,000.00;

(b) Pre-judgment interest pursuant to the *Judgment Interest Act*, S.A. 1984, c. J-0.5;

(c) Costs;

(d) Such further and other relief as this Honourable Court deems just.

DATED at the City of [**Place**], in the Province of Alberta, this * day of *, A.D. 19*, AND DELIVERED BY [**Law Firm Name**], Barristers and Solicitors, Solicitors for the Plaintiff herein whose address for service is in care of the said Solicitors, [**Address**], [**Place**], Alberta, [**Postal Code**].

ISSUED out of the office of the Clerk of this Honourable Court this * day of *, A.D. 19*.

_____
Clerk of the Court

NOTICE

TO [Name of Defendant]

You have been sued. You are the Defendant. You have only 15 days to file and serve a Statement of Defence or Demand of Notice. You or your lawyer must file your Statement of Defence or Demand of Notice in the office of the Clerk of the Court of Queen's Bench in **[Place]**, Alberta. You or your lawyer must also leave a copy of your Statement of Defence or Demand of Notice at the address for service for the Plaintiff named in this Statement of Claim.

WARNING: If you do not do both things within 15 days, you may automatically lose the lawsuit. The Plaintiff may get a Court Judgment against you if you do not file, or do not give a copy to the Plaintiff, or do either thing late.

This Statement of Claim is issued by

NAME OF LAW FIRM
Lawyer's Name
File No. *
Telephone No. *
Fax No. *

Solicitors for the Plaintiff whose address for service is in care of the said solicitors.

The Plaintiff resides at *

The Defendant (so far as known to the Plaintiff) resides at *

ACTION NO. *

IN THE COURT OF QUEEN'S
BENCH OF ALBERTA
JUDICIAL CENTRE OF *

BETWEEN:

*

Plaintiff

- and -

*

Defendant

STATEMENT OF CLAIM

Agent:

*

LAW FIRM NAME
Barristers and Solicitors
* Address
* Place, Alberta
* Postal Code

APPENDIX 2H
Reasonable Notice Periods – Alberta Cases

I. Senior Executives

	CASE	POSITION	AGE	SALARY	LENGTH OF SERVICE	LENGTH OF UNEMP'T	NOTICE PERIOD
1.	*McGuire v. Wardair Canada Ltd.* (1970), 71 W.W.R. 705 (Alta. T.D.)	Vice President and General Manager	–	$20,500 + share options	3 years	6 months	12 months
2.	*Rivest v. Canfarge Ltd.*, [1977] 4 W.W.R. 515 (Alta. T.D.)	Vice President and General Manager	46	$31,800 + bonus	19 years	2 years	12 months
3.	*Bagby v. Gustavson International Drilling Co.* (1979), 20 A.R. 244 (T.D.), varied (1980), 24 A.R. 181 (C.A.)	Chief Executive Officer	–	$72,000 + bonus	24 years	–	15 months
4.	*Dixon v. Merland Exploration Ltd.* (1984), 30 Alta L.R. (2d) 310 (Q.B.)	President	53	$170,000 + bonuses	6 years	–	18 months
5.	*Olson v. Sprung Instant Greenhouses Ltd.* (1985), 41 Alta. L.R. (2d) 325 (Q.B.)	General Manager and Chief Executive Officer	35	$57,000	7 years	13 months	8 months
6.	*Farrugia v. Ashland Oil Canada Ltd.* (1986), 75 A.R. 11 (Q.B.)	Divisional Vice President	–	$35,561 + bonus	24 years	–	15 months
7.	*PCM Construction Control Consultants Ltd. v. Heeger* (1989), 97 A.R. 24 (Q.B.)	Director	–	$49,000	4 1/2 years	6 months	9 months
8.	*Walsh v. Alberta & Southern Gas Co.* (1991), 84 Alta. L.R. (2d) 75 (Q.B.)	Vice President	49	$110,000	8 1/2 years	–	15 months
9.	*Burns v. Oxford Development Group Inc.* (1992), 128 A.R. 345 (Q.B.)	Senior Vice President, Alta.	56	$225,000 + bonuses	18 months	2 years	at least 12 months

	CASE	POSITION	AGE	SALARY	LENGTH OF SERVICE	LENGTH OF UNEMP'T	NOTICE PERIOD
10.	*Morrison v. Alberta Distillers Ltd.* (1994), 3 C.C.E.L. (2d) 241 (Alta. Q.B.)	Head, Technical Services	62		27 years	at least 1 year, 3 months	18 months

II. Upper Management

	CASE	POSITION	AGE	SALARY	LENGTH OF SERVICE	LENGTH OF UNEMP'T	NOTICE PERIOD
11.	*Muhlenfeld v. Northern Alberta Rapeseed Producers' Co-operative Ltd.* (1980), 13 Alta. L.R. (2d) 105 (Q.B.)	Project Manager	49	$46,000	2 years	2 months	12 months
12.	*MacLeod v. Geoservices North America Ltd.* (1983), 44 A.R. 93 (Q.B.)	General Manager	31	$26,400	7 1/2 years	–	8 months
		Area Manager	31	$19,800	2 years	–	6 months
13.	*Wilcox v. G.W.G. Ltd.* (1984), [1984] 4 W.W.R. 70 (Alta. Q.B.), reversed (1985), [1986] 1 W.W.R. 567 (C.A.)	Director of Operations (similar to Vice President)	50's		4 years	–	2 months (reduced from 10-12 months' notice due to near cause)
14.	*Johnston v. Canada Cement Lafarge Ltd.* (1984), 12 C.C.E.L. 108 (Alta. C.A.)	General Manager (Engineer)	–	$76,650	26 years	at least 12 months	24 months
15.	*Ibrahim v. Assn. of Professional Engineers, Geologists & Geophysicists of Alberta* (1985), 41 Alta. L.R. (2d) 126 (Q.B.)	Director of Communications (Professional Engineer)	55	$46,000	3 years, 7 months	20 months	12 months
16.	*Fisher v. Calgary (City)* (1986), 48 Alta. L.R. (2d) 35 (C.A.)	Senior Managerial Position	58		18 months	–	9 months
17.	*Lacroix v. Esso Resources Canada Ltd.* (1988), 85 A.R. 313 (Q.B.)	Superintendent of Construction and Support Operations	48		12 years	–	18 months

86

III. Middle Management

	CASE	POSITION	AGE	SALARY	LENGTH OF SERVICE	LENGTH OF UNEMP'T	NOTICE PERIOD
18.	*Vos v. Security Trust Co.* (1969), 68 W.W.R. 310 (Alta. T.D.)	Assistant General Manager	40	$15,000	14 years	–	6 months
19.	*Shtabsky v. Dubeta* (1974), [1974] 4 W.W.R. 324 (Alta. T.D.)	Manager	–	$12,000	2 weeks	1 week	12 months
20.	*Colgan v. Blackfoot Motor Inn Ltd.* (1976), 2 A.R. 258 (T.D.)	Hotel Manager	–	$12,000	2 months	10 months	8 months
21.	*Floen v. Farmers & Merchants Trust Co.* (1977), 5 A.R. 249 (T.D.)	Branch Manager	–	$15,000	3 1/2 years	–	8 months
22.	*Clark v. Faber* (1977), 6 A.R. 415 (T.D.)	Office Manager	–	$19,800	4 years	8 months	8 months
23.	*Mack v. Link Hardware Co.* (1978), 92 D.L.R. (3d) 757 (Alta. Dist. Ct.)	Advertising Manager	33	$15,756	7 years	2 months	4 months
24.	*Veilleux v. Phoenix Paper Products Ltd.* (1978), 20 A.R. 110 (T.D.)	Branch Manager	–	$16,900	1 1/2 years	–	6 months
25.	*O'Regan v. Alger* (1978), 12 A.R. 361 (T.D.)	Office Manager	–	$12,000	7 weeks	1 1/2 months	1 month
26.	*Smith v. Tamblyn (Alberta) Ltd.* (1979), 9 Alta. L.R. (2d) 274 (T.D.)	Pharmacist-Assistant Manager	–		7 years	23 months	9 months
27.	*Kunz v. Liggett Drug Ltd.* (1981), 36 A.R. 299 (Q.B.)	Pharmacist Manager	–	$20,600	4 1/2 years	–	9 months
28.	*Wilcox v. G.W.G. Ltd.*, [1984] 4 W.W.R. 70 (Alta. Q.B.), reversed (1985), [1986] 1 W.W.R. 567 (Alta. C.A.)	General Productions Manager	50's		14 years	–	1 year reduced to 4 months (near cause)

	CASE	POSITION	AGE	SALARY	LENGTH OF SERVICE	LENGTH OF UNEMP'T	NOTICE PERIOD
29.	*Kowton v. Edmonton (City)* (1985), 38 Alta. L.R. (2d) 397 (Q.B.)	Land Audit and Transfer Manager	58	$49,400	17 1/2 years	at least 19 months	15 months
30.	*Tabone v. Midas Canada Inc.* (1986), 46 Alta. L.R. (2d) 238 (Q.B.)	Store Manager	50	$29,000	18 years	–	12 months
31.	*Lock v. Bovis Dental Laboratory Ltd.* (1986), 2 A.C.W.S. (3d) 210 (Alta. Q.B.)	General Manager	–	$26,808	9 years	6 weeks	6 months
32.	*Merryweather v. Browning-Ferris Industries Ltd.* (1986), 75 A.R. 275 (Q.B.), reversed (April 14, 1988), Doc. Calgary Appeal AC-01-19096 (C.A.)	District Manager	43	$32,000	11 years	–	6 months
33.	*Elliott v. Southam Inc.* (1988), 59 Alta. L.R. (2d) 376 (Q.B.)	Systems Manager	47		22 years	at least 18 months	15 months
34.	*D'Onofrio v. Dowell Schlumberger Canada Inc.* (1988), 94 A.R. 34 (Q.B.)	Service Superintendent	43	$44,000	15 years	–	8 months
35.	*Davidson v. Vulcan Machinery & Equipment* (1988), 90 A.R. 342 (Q.B.)	Manager	52	$45,000	5 years	–	8 months
36.	*English v. NBI Canada Inc.* (1989), 92 A.R. 225 (Q.B.)	Branch Manager	47	$27,600	2 years	–	4 months
37.	*Carr v. Ireco Canada II Inc.* (1991), 80 Alta. L.R. (2d) 154 (Q.B.)	Regional Manager	48	$59,615	21 years	at least 20 months	15 months
38.	*Cunningham Estate v. Stahl Diesel Sales Ltd.* (1991), 83 Alta. L.R. (2d) 184 (C.A.)	Middle Manager	–		5 years	–	12 months at trial (reduced to 6 months)
39.	*Hill v. Dow Chemical Canada Inc.* (1993), 11 Alta. L.R. (3d) 66 (Q.B.)	Security Superintendent	48	$65,460	7 years	10 months	11 months

	CASE	POSITION	AGE	SALARY	LENGTH OF SERVICE	LENGTH OF UNEMP'T	NOTICE PERIOD
40.	*PCL Construction Management Inc. v. Holmes Inc.* (1994), [1995] 3 W.W.R. 502 (Alta. C.A.)	Project Manager	55	–	15 years	–	12 months
41.	*Zimmermann v. Calgary District Hospital Group* (1994), 26 Alta. L.R. (2d) 365 (Q.B.)	Manager of Respiratory Services	55	$48,626	32 years	–	18 months
42.	*Schmidt v. Sears Canada Inc.* (1995), 12 C.C.E.L. (2d) 261 (Alta. Q.B.)	Store Manager	44	$71,000	24 years	–	12 months

IV. Lower Management

	CASE	POSITION	AGE	SALARY	LENGTH OF SERVICE	LENGTH OF UNEMP'T	NOTICE PERIOD
43.	*Athwal v. Edmonton (City)* (1986), 47 Alta. L.R. (2d) 174 (C.A.)	Junior Manager	62		4 years	–	13 months (date at which pension would vest considered)
44.	*Boleszczuk v. South Centre Fine Cars Ltd.* (1991), 38 C.C.E.L. 193 (Alta. Prov. Ct.)	Service Manager	young	$34,684	10 1/2 months	3 months	3 weeks
45.	*Christianson v. North Hill News Inc.* (1992), 1 Alta. L.R. (3d) 110 (Q.B.), reversed in part (1993), 13 Alta. L.R. (3d) 78 (C.A.)	Assistant Manager, Composing Room Supervisor	43	$38,000	17 years	at least 14 months	6 months (12 months on appeal)
46.	*Taylor v. Dallas Investments Inc.* (1993), 8 Alta. L.R. (3d) 181 (Q.B.)	Manager	46	$39,600	6 years, 7 months	–	6 months
47.	*Reeves v. GAP International Inc.* (1995), 10 C.C.E.L. (2d) 262 (Alta. Prov. Ct.)	Store Manager	35	–	1 year, 8 months	–	1 1/2-2 years

V. Foremen and Supervisors

	CASE	POSITION	AGE	SALARY	LENGTH OF SERVICE	LENGTH OF UNEMP'T	NOTICE PERIOD
48.	*Wright v. Calgary Auxiliary Hospital & Nursing Home* (1971), [1971] 1 W.W.R. 532 (Alta. T.D.)	Supervisor of Wash-Floor	55	$5,000	9 years	–	6 months
49.	*Vlooswyck v. Elevator Builders Construction Ltd.* (1978), 11 A.R. 388 (T.D.)	Supervisor	–		1 1/2 years	1 month	3 months
50.	*Salmi v. Greyfriar Developments Ltd.* (1983), 27 Alta. L.R. (2d) 204 (Q.B.), reversed in part (1985), 36 Alta. L.R. (2d) 182 (C.A.)	Construction Supervisor	–	$35,000	10 months	–	2 months
51.	*Zimmer v. Cascade Construction Ltd.* (1985), 39 Alta. L.R. (2d) 66 (Q.B.)	Construction Superin-tendent	49	$40,200	1 1/2 years	–	3 months
52.	*Copses v. Kraft Con-struction (1978) Ltd.* (1986), 48 Alta. L.R. (2d) 180 (Q.B.)	Job Superin-tendent	–	$38,400	10 months	7 months	3 months
53.	*Clark v. Fiberglas Canada Inc.* (1993), 7 Alta. L.R. (3d) 426 (Q.B.)	Shift Super-visor	62	$63,700	31 years	at least 16 months but mitigation not a factor	22 months
54.	*Birch v. Southam Inc.* (1993), 9 Alta. L.R. (3d) 187 (Q.B.)	Assistant Supervisor			14 years	at least 16 months	10 months
55.	*Ganam v. Con-solidated Concrete Ltd.* (1993), 8 Alta. L.R. (3d) 288 (C.A.)	Quality Con-trol Super-visor	–		5 years, leave of absence to pursue degree	–	9 months

VI. Professionals

	CASE	POSITION	AGE	SALARY	LENGTH OF SERVICE	LENGTH OF UNEMP'T	NOTICE PERIOD
56.	*Allison v. Amoco Production Co.* (1975), 58 D.L.R. (3d) 233 (Alta. T.D.)	District Geophysicist	–	$40,000	25 years	–	12 months
57.	*Lukey v. SNC Consultants Ltd.* (unreported, October 12, 1983, Alta. Q.B.)	Head, Civil Engineering Department	mid-50's		6 years	–	6 months
58.	*House of Light Ltd. v. Cunningham* (1985), 12 C.C.E.L. 97 (Alta. C.A.)	Chartered Accountant	–	$46,600 + benefits	4 years	12 months	12 months (reduced to 8 months on appeal for failure to mitigate)
59.	*Newell v. Leasametric (Canada) Inc.* (1986), 46 Alta. L.R. (2d) 397 (Q.B.)	Staff Engineer (Sales)	–	$30,500	10 months	7 months	4 months
60.	*Adams v. Coseka Resources Ltd.* (1988), 22 C.C.E.L. 164 (Alta. Q.B.)	Corporate Counsel	–	$70,000	13 months	9 months	5 months
61.	*Rahmath v. Louisiana Land & Exploration Co.* (1989), 59 D.L.R. (4th) 606 (Alta. C.A.), additional reasons (1989), 65 D.L.R. (4th) 150 (Alta. C.A.)	"Skilled Professional"	37	$60,000	2 years	–	4 months
62.	*Pagnotta v. Read Jones Christoffersen Ltd.* (1990), 29 C.C.E.L. 5 (Alta. Q.B.)	Design Engineer	29	$30,600	8 years	14 months	7 months
63.	*Barefoot v. R.R.S. Howard Professional Corp.* (1991), 36 C.C.E.L. 278 (Alta. Q.B.)	Doctor	–	$84,000	5 months	4 months	4 months
64.	*Edwards v. Royal Alexandra Hospital* (1994), 5 C.C.E.L. (2d) 196 (Alta. Q.B.)	Obstetrics Unit Manager (Nurse)	56	$53,643 + benefits	36 years (less 4 years – break in service)	–	21 months

VII. Education Employees

	CASE	POSITION	AGE	SALARY	LENGTH OF SERVICE	LENGTH OF UNEMP'T	NOTICE PERIOD
65.	*Glass v. Warner County School Committee* (1979), 17 A.R. 313 (Dist. Ct.)	Vice Principal	–		15 years	–	4 months

VIII. Administrators

	CASE	POSITION	AGE	SALARY	LENGTH OF SERVICE	LENGTH OF UNEMP'T	NOTICE PERIOD
66.	*Baker v. United Grain Growers Ltd.* (1978), [1978] 5 W.W.R. 370 (Alta. T.D.)	Field Services Coordinator	51	$20,160	26 years	7 months	12 months
67.	*Ratsoy v. West End Day Care Society* (1978), 13 A.R. 545 (Dist. Ct.)	Director, Childcare Centre	31	$14,400	6 years	–	8 months
68.	*Knapp v. Baker Lovick*, [1979] 1 A.C.W.S. 139	Associate Creative Director	41		1 year	–	6 months
69.	*Coyes v. Ocelot Industries Ltd.* (1984), 33 Alta. L.R. (2d) 102 (Q.B.)	Materials Coordinator	25	$28,800	3 1/2 years	–	1 month
70.	*Matthewson v. Aiton Power Ltd.* (1984), 3 C.C.E.L. 69, reversed (1985), 8 C.C.E.L. 312 (Ont. C.A.)	Chief Estimator	–	$37,000	3 years	6 months	8 months
71.	*Molavi v. S.H. Chandler Architect Ltd.* (1984), 54 A.R. 241 (C.A.)	Contract Administrator	39	$36,000	9 months	–	3 months
72.	*Zylawy v. Edmonton (City)* (1985), 8 C.C.E.L. 93 (Alta. Q.B.)	Supervisor of Space, Planning & Co-ordination	38	$48,000	2 years	9 months	8 months
73.	*Parish v. Alberta* (1987), 81 A.R. 306 (Q.B.)	Executive Director, Program Development	56		5 years	–	10 months

	CASE	POSITION	AGE	SALARY	LENGTH OF SERVICE	LENGTH OF UNEMP'T	NOTICE PERIOD
74.	*McGarry v. Bosco Homes Edmonton* (1992), 42 C.C.E.L. 198 (Alta. Q.B.)	Office/ Personnel Manager	47	$35,000	2 1/4 years	–	6 months

IX. Sales/Marketing Employees and Managers

	CASE	POSITION	AGE	SALARY	LENGTH OF SERVICE	LENGTH OF UNEMP'T	NOTICE PERIOD
75.	*Hardie v. Trans-Canada Resources Ltd.* (1976), 71 D.L.R. (3d) 668 (Alta. C.A.)	Salesman	–	$29,000	14 years	–	20 months
76.	*Hunt v. Cimco Ltd.* (1976), 2 A.R. 514 (T.D.)	Salesman	–	$12,000	7 years	–	6 months
77.	*Raypold v. McEvoy Oilfield Services* (1977), 2 A.R. 134 (T.D.)	Sales Manager	–		18 years	–	10 months
78.	*Aleniuk v. Westown Ford Sales Ltd.* (1981), 28 A.R. 473 (Q.B.)	Sales Manager	37	$46,800	2 1/2 years	1 year	6 months
79.	*Busch v. GTE Sylvania Canada Ltd.* (1982), 40 A.R. 189 (C.A.)	Senior Salesman	54	$28,000	10 years	–	9 months
80.	*Kokonis v. Shaw Pipe Industries Ltd.* (1982), 41 A.R. 140 (Q.B.)	Senior Sales Manager	42	$56,000	13 years	–	12 months
81.	*Denhoff v. B & L Lumber Ltd.* (1987), 53 Alta. L.R. (2d) 300 (Q.B.)	Lumber Salesman	30	$53,000	2 years	14 months	4 months
82.	*McMaster v. Dresser Canada Inc.* (1989), 30 C.C.E.L. 132 (Alta. Q.B.)	Sales Employee	52	$54,000	9 months + previous 9 years	5 months	6 months
83.	*Beaudoin v. Canadian Corporate News Inc.* (1989), 32 C.C.E.L. 84 (Alta. Q.B.)	Salesman	–		2 years	–	3 months (near cause)

	CASE	POSITION	AGE	SALARY	LENGTH OF SERVICE	LENGTH OF UNEMP'T	NOTICE PERIOD
84.	*Hourie v. Joseph E. Seagram & Sons Ltd.* (1990), 106 A.R. 231 (Q.B.)	District Sales Repre- sentative	52	$32,520	20 years	–	12 months
85.	*Farmer v. Foxridge Homes Ltd.* (1992), 6 Alta. L.R. (3d) 150, reversed in part (1994), 18 Alta. L.R. (3d) 182 (C.A.)	Sales Manager	56	$169,515	4 years	6 weeks	12 months
86.	*Dash v. Hudson Bay Co.* (1992), [1992] 5 W.W.R. 501 (Alta. Q.B.)	Salesman	37	$48,000	10 years	4 months	6 months
87.	*Blackmore v. Cablenet Ltd.* (1994), 26 Alta. L.R. (3d) 108 (Q.B.)	Marketing Representa- tive	–	$120,000 (comm.)	3 years	–	4 months

X. Technical and Skilled Employees

	CASE	POSITION	AGE	SALARY	LENGTH OF SERVICE	LENGTH OF UNEMP'T	NOTICE PERIOD
88.	*Chadburn v. Sinclair Canada Oil Co.* (1966), 57 W.W.R. 477 (Alta. T.D.)	Senior Em- ployee of Land Department	53		11 years	–	6 months
89.	*Thiessen v. Leduc* (1975), [1975] 4 W.W.R. 387 (Alta. T.D.)	Chief Con- stable	39	$8,160	3 years	7 months	10 months
90.	*Frost v. Montreal En- gineering Co.* (1983), 3 C.C.E.L. 86 (Alta. Q.B.)	Senior Tech- nical Assistant/ Designer	39	$42,000	6 years, 8 months	at least 15 months	8 months
91.	*Henze v. Kamor Fur- niture Ltd.* (1985), 39 Alta. L.R. (2d) 343 (Q.B.)	Upholsterer	43	$27,500	8 years	3 months	8 months (reduced to 3 months) (near cause)
92.	*Sarton v. Fluor Can- ada Ltd.* (1986), 73 A.R. 241 (C.A.)	Engineering Draftsman	–	$46,200	2 years	approx. 6 months	4 months

	CASE	POSITION	AGE	SALARY	LENGTH OF SERVICE	LENGTH OF UNEMP'T	NOTICE PERIOD
93.	*Visentin v. Shell Canada Ltd.* (1989), 29 C.C.E.L. 65 (Alta. Q.B.)	Gas Field Operator	–	$32,528	7 years	–	6 months
94.	*Miller v. Petro-Canada* (1992), 44 C.C.E.L. 230 (Alta. Q.B.)	Operations Analyst	–	$41,100	8 years, 8 months	–	8 months

XI. Clerical Employees

	CASE	POSITION	AGE	SALARY	LENGTH OF SERVICE	LENGTH OF UNEMP'T	NOTICE PERIOD
95.	*Wadden v. Guaranty Trust Co. of Canada* (1987), 49 Alta. L.R. (2d) 348 (Q.B.)	Loans Clerk	44	$20,628	2 years, 3 months	21 months	6 months
96.	*Heinz v. Cana Construction Co. Ltd.* (1987), 55 Alta. L.R. (2d) 382 (Q.B.)	Equipment Clerk	56	$38,400	31 years	at least 1 1/2 years	12 months
97.	*Wilkinson v. T. Eaton Co.* (1992), 41 C.C.E.L. 57 (Alta. Q.B.), affirmed (1992), 44 C.C.E.L. 287 (Alta. C.A.)	Clerk-Typist	65		43 years	–	18 months

XII. Labourers

	CASE	POSITION	AGE	SALARY	LENGTH OF SERVICE	LENGTH OF UNEMP'T	NOTICE PERIOD
98.	*Jivrag v. Calgary (City)* (1986), 13 C.C.E.L. 120 (Q.B.), varied (1987), 18 C.C.E.L. xxx (C.A.)	Parking Lot Attendant	52		5 years	–	6 months
99.	*Conway v. George's Farm Centre Ltd.* (1986), 44 Alta. L.R. (2d) 115 (Q.B.)	Partsman	32	$44,920	8 years	8 1/2 months	8 months
100.	*Morrissey v. Whyte Avenue Hotel Co.* (1989), 98 A.R. 219 (Q.B.)	Bartender	30	$10,000 + tips	3 1/2 years	–	13 weeks

	CASE	POSITION	AGE	SALARY	LENGTH OF SERVICE	LENGTH OF UNEMP'T	NOTICE PERIOD
101.	*Spencer v. Tim Horton's* (1995), 10 C.C.E.L. (2d) 298 (Alta. Prov. Ct.)	Bus Driver	52	–	4 years	–	2 months
102.	*Lay v. Jaffary* (1995), [1995] 7 W.W.R. 465 (Alta. Q.B.)	Ranchhand	–	$21,000	1 year	–	1 1/2 months

XIII. Miscellaneous Employees

	CASE	POSITION	AGE	SALARY	LENGTH OF SERVICE	LENGTH OF UNEMP'T	NOTICE PERIOD
103.	*Benson v. Lynes United Services Ltd.* (1979), 18 A.R. 328 (T.D.)	Trainee	30	$7,800	5 1/2 months	–	3 months
104.	*Brown v. Fidinam (Canada) Ltd.* (1980), 23 A.R. 608 (Q.B.)	Apartment Superin-tendent	–	$8,100	10 months	–	12 months
105.	*Fletcher v. Cliffcrest Enterprises Ltd.* (1985), 9 C.C.E.L. 45 (Alta. Q.B.)	Personnel Recruiter	–		6 years	–	7 months
106.	*Allen v. International Union, U.M.W.A.* (1987), 52 Alta. L.R. (2d) 386 (Q.B.)	Employee Union Or-ganizer	–		3 1/2 years	2 months	6 months
107.	*Chettleborough v. Canadian Concrete Products Ltd.* (1988), 85 A.R. 234 (Q.B.)	Chief Dis-patcher	38	$40,080	8 years	–	7 months
108.	*Ambler v. J. Gilmour Interiors Inc.* (1992), 6 Alta. L.R. (3d) 176 (Q.B.)	Design Con-sultant	young		16 months	–	5 months

APPENDIX 2I

Wrongful Dismissal Litigation Timeline – Plaintiff

ACTING FOR THE PLAINTIFF

1. Draft Demand Letter – Diarize for 7 days after demand letter sent.

2. Conduct Corporate Search of parties.

3. If demand letter not responded to, prepare draft Statement of Claim.

4. Following review by lawyer, review Statement of Claim with client over the telephone and confirm it is correct – confirm instructions to file.

5. File and serve Statement of Claim as follows:

Unrepresented defendants

(a) Corporate Defendant's registered office by single registered mail.

(b) Individuals by process server.

Represented defendants

(a) Serve through legal counsel – get to admit service and undertake to defend. – Follow up regularly to ensure this is done with phone calls and letters.

6. If no Statement of Defence received – do as follows:

Unrepresented parties

(a) 15 days after personal service.

(b) 22 days after posting by single registered mail, file and serve Note in Default.

Represented parties

(a) 15 days after receipt of solicitor's acknowledgment and under-taking to defend, bring application for Default Judgment under appro-priate Rule of Court.

8. Once Defence received, prepare, file and serve Demand for Discovery and Notice to Produce.

9. Prepare draft Affidavit of Documents and Production:

(a) Letter to client re producible documents;

(b) Photocopy and organize producible documents Copies: client, other side, working copies; and

(c) Original documents to be retained in separate folio.

10. Send standard letter enclosing draft Affidavit and producible documents to other counsel (cc. client).

11. Request other parties' draft Affidavit and copies of producible documents.

12. Schedule Examinations for Discovery:

(a) Phone other parties for dates;

(b) Check with client – also book preparation appointment with client;

(c) Book Court Reporter;

(d) Send confirming letters to other parties and client; and

(e) Make sure conference room is booked if Discovery held here.

13. Forward standard Examination for Discovery letter to client confirming dates and preparation appointment.

14. Complete preparation of trial book and have reviewed by lawyer.

15. Trial book and file to lawyer at least one day in advance of Examination For Discovery to ensure preparation.

16. After Discovery, include Discovery Exhibits, counsel notes, etc., in trial book – Make sure trial book up-to-date.

17. Forward copies of transcripts to client for review and comment with covering letter. Ask client to complete responses to undertakings as soon as possible.

18. Diarize for follow-up.

19. Place original transcripts in separate folio. Punched copies to be put in trial book.

20. Write to opposing counsel requesting responses to undertakings in 30 days (or longer if lawyer requires).

21. Phone opposing counsel re responses to undertakings. If not available, prepare application to compel response.

22. When undertakings arrive:

    (a) Lawyer to review;

    (b) Response to be placed in trial book;

    (c) Copy to file; and

    (d) Copy of Undertakings to be forwarded to client for review and comment.

23. Prepare and sign Certificate of Readiness and forward to opposing counsel – Follow-up with opposing counsel to ensure that it is signed in a timely fashion.

24. File Certificate of Readiness and Record to set trial date.

25. Schedule pre-trial if required.

26. Send standard letter to client regarding trial date and procedure.

27. Lawyer to review file for trial preparation.

28. Set appointments for trial preparation for client and witnesses.

3

REPRESENTING EMPLOYERS

3.1 INTRODUCTION

o In representing employers, the objective is to discharge the employee either for cause, or upon reasonable notice, minimizing liability through litigation and minimizing liability for legal fees.

o In the case of a dismissal without cause, the objective is to arrive at a fair severance package in accordance with legal principles.

3.2 INITIAL CONSULTATION

o The initial consultation may take place by telephone or a meeting. In many cases, once consideration has been given to termination of employment of one or more employees, the client wishes to proceed in the most expeditious fashion so as to implement the decision quickly and with minimal disruption to the workplace.

3.2.1 INDIVIDUAL TERMINATION OF EMPLOYMENT

(a) General

o Fully discuss reasons for termination with client.

o Is there just cause for summary dismissal? See Section 3.3, *infra*.

Note:
> In "grey cases" the client may wish to waive summary dismissal for cause and provide some reasonable notice.

o Review the employee's background, whether he or she was enticed from a previously secure position, hiring, position and duties, salary, age, supervisorial responsibilities, length of service, etc.

o Determine whether there is any employment contract, collective agreement, or applicable policies that may apply. If necessary, obtain the documentation and review it.

o Provide the client with preliminary evaluation of reasonable notice and the range of damages.

o Advise the client of the employee's duty to mitigate and the impact of damages and strategy. Obtain an assessment from the client as to alternative job opportunities for this particular employee.

o Determine final pay and employment standards considerations.

(b)   Unemployment Benefits Considerations

o Record of Employment – This must be issued promptly: include the reason for termination and be consistent with the approach on the dismissal.

o Consider the impact of the reasons for termination on the employees entitlement to unemployment benefits: i.e., if the employee resigns or is dismissed for wilful misconduct he or she may be disqualified from benefits.

o If the employee is offered part-time or casual employment leading up to the unemployment benefits claim, this may detrimentally affect the unemployment benefits entitlement.

o The employee will be disqualified for benefits if he or she loses employment due to wilful misconduct. If the cause for dismissal is shown on the Record of Employment, the employer will be obligated to respond to the commission's request for further information, including full details of dismissal, so that an evaluation can be made.

o If the employer disagrees with the conclusion of the commission regarding entitlement, the employer has a right of appeal to the Board of Referees or umpire. See: *Employment Insurance Act*, S.C. 1996, c. 23, ss. 114 and 115.

(c) W.C.B./Disability Issues

o If the employee has had an industrial accident, the employer is obligated to file notice to W.C.B.. While termination of employment will not affect entitlement to W.C.B. coverage, because the employee does not have a job to go back to the period of rehabilitation could be much longer. The cost of the claim will be charged to the employer's experience record.

o With respect to a disability, the employer may be contractually obligated to provide short-term or long-term disability benefits.

o In the case of termination of employment, the employer will want to ensure that termination of employment does not affect the entitlement to claim disability benefits. Otherwise the employer could be liable for disability benefits during the period of total disability up to age 65.

o If there is any issue as to disability entitlement, the employer should phone the disability carrier to determine whether the termination of employment will affect disability coverage.

o This should be fully reviewed with legal counsel prior to making a final decision as to termination of employment.

(d)   Benefits and Pension

o The employer has the option of continuing benefits over the period of reasonable notice (or until other employment is obtained) or providing compensation for loss of benefits.

(i)   Continuing benefits

o The advantage of continuing benefits is that it eliminates the risks associated with any benefit claims.

o However, some benefits carriers will not provide benefits coverage for an employee who is no longer actively at work even though the premiums have been paid. This must be determined from the benefits carrier in advance.

o The other disadvantage of continuing benefits is that it may encourage the employee to go on disability during part of the period of reasonable notice. According to the decisions of some courts, this suspends the period of reasonable notice.

(ii)   Providing compensation

o The other alternative is to provide for compensation for loss of benefits. This usually equates to the employer's cost of providing those benefits over the period of reasonable notice.

o Some employers prefer to offer salary only over the period of reasonable notice even though the employee is entitled to compensation for loss of benefits.

(e)   Outplacement Counselling

o In the case of an employee who has been dismissed, either with or without cause, the employer may wish to consider providing outplacement counselling to assist the employee in obtaining alternative employment.

o Giving assistance in searching for new employment may assist the employee in mitigating his or her damages and thereby lower the ultimate cost to the employer.

3.2.2 DOWNSIZING OR CORPORATE RESTRUCTURING

o Employees discharged through a downsizing or corporate restructuring have been dismissed without cause. Where this involves a large number of employees, careful planning must take place in advance.

o Ask the client in advance to provide details pertaining to employees to be discharged, including name, title, duties, age, length of service and salary.

o Consider any contractual documents or severance policy.

o Consider the pros and cons of a voluntary severance arrangement. However, the employer should note that the employer then has little control over who leaves the workplace and usually the better employees will take a voluntary severance package.

o Make an assessment of periods of reasonable notice and damages for each employee to be discharged. Consider putting this into the table format for review by the client.

o Consider whether a fair severance formula can be applied universally to all employees.

o Prepare a draft severance package and review with the client.

o Consider use of outplacement counsellor. You may wish to retain the outplacement counsellor to be present when packages are presented to employees and to provide initial information.

o Contact the Canada Employment and Immigration Commission office and determine whether someone is available to make a presentation at the workplace to advise employees as to unemployment benefit entitlement and to assist in making claims.

o Determine the timing for finalizing severance packages, preparing all the relevant documentation, and implementing the severance.

o Consider counselling for those employees who remain following a corporate downsizing or restructuring, which will have a detrimental impact on employee morale and will certainly affect the employees' sense of job security.

o Consider a negotiation strategy. In the cases of a large downsizing or corporate restructuring, given the number of employees involved, adjustment of the severance package for one employee may result in demands from other employees whose severance offer is outstanding.

3.3   JUST CAUSE AND OTHER DEFENCES

o Fully review the situation to determine whether just cause exists for summary dismissal, or whether other available defences to the case exist.

o In cases of incompetence, determine whether:
  o Standards were reasonable and were clearly articulated.
  o Warnings were given.
  o Assistance and a reasonable opportunity to improve were provided.
  o The employee was advised that if improvement not noted, it will result in discharge for cause.

o If cause is not clear, consider termination for cause together with a "without prejudice" offer. Alternatively, the employer may wish to waive the right to terminate for cause and offer some severance package.

o If the employer wishes to allege cause, then the employee should be dismissed summarily; that is, there should be no offer of notice or pay in lieu of notice.

Note:
The requirement to provide reasonable notice, or pay in lieu of, pursuant to the *Employment Standards Code* ("*E.S.C.*"), S.A. 1988, c. E-10.2, does not apply in the case of dismissal for cause. See: s. 58(l)(e).

o The allegations as to cause must be genuine. Where improper allegations of cause have been made and later disproved, this can result in a significantly higher damages award, aggravated or punitive damages, and possibly solicitor and client costs. See: *Dixon v. British Columbia Transit* (1995), 13 C.C.E.L. (2d) 272 (S.C.), additional reasons at (1995), 15 C.C.E.L. (2d) 290 (S.C.).

3.4   REVIEW OF DOCUMENTATION

o Following the initial consultation, the employer should be requested to forward all relevant documentation and the employee's personnel file to legal counsel for review.

o Documentation should include any employment contract, signed statements, relevant policies, etc.

3.5   PUTTING TOGETHER AND PRESENTING THE PACKAGE

3.5.1   THE PACKAGE

o Agreement should be reached as to whether the employer or legal counsel will prepare the draft package. Regardless, the package should be reviewed so that both the employer and legal counsel are comfortable with it.

o The notice of termination together with any severance package should be presented at a brief meeting involving at least two representatives of management and the employee. See: Section 3.7: Tactical Considerations and Strategies.

3.5.2 THE TERMINATION INTERVIEW

o Usually two people from management should be present to verify what took place. The interview should be brief and to the point.

o Briefly outline the reasons for termination of employment and advise that the decision is irrevocable.

o Present the package and ask the employee to reply within the deadline which has been set. After expressing regret, thank the employee for his service to the company and wish him every success in his or her future endeavours (if that is appropriate).

o Offer the employee any assistance.

o Have someone escort the employee to his or her office or work space to gather any personal belongings and leave the workplace as soon as possible. Ideally, termination of employment should take place at the beginning of the week so that the employee has the opportunity to obtain independent legal and financial advice.

o Employers should be discouraged from terminating employees prior to major holiday periods.

o Counsel should offer to prepare the letter of termination of employment and the severance package to be presented to the employee, or alternatively offer to review it.

3.6 OUTPLACEMENT COUNSELLING

o The employer should seriously consider offering outplacement counselling to discharged employees to assist them in obtaining alternative employment at the earliest possible opportunity.

o Outplacement firms offer a variety and full range of programs to assist employees who have lost their jobs. These include counselling for the individual and family members to deal with the uncertainty and stress of unemployment. It also includes résumé preparation, job search strategies, networking, the use of an office, and other programs.

o Outplacement counselling can be of tremendous benefit to some former employees, particularly those in a difficult job market or those who have been out of the job search market for a long period of time.

o For those employees who have a broad job market, the programs offered through the Canada Employment and Immigration Centre may be satisfactory, and therefore these employees may not benefit from a broader range of outplacement services.

o Before committing to outplacement counselling or an outplacement firm, employers should survey all of the firms in their geographic area, and compare their programs and fees to determine which is most suitable.

o Where outplacement counselling is offered by the employer to the departing employee, the program should be offered and paid for irrespective of whether the employee accepts the severance package or not. The objective is to assist the employee in dealing with his or her uncertain circumstances and to assist them in obtaining employment as quickly as possible.

3.7 TACTICAL CONSIDERATIONS AND STRATEGIES

3.7.1 DISMISSAL FOR CAUSE

o In a dismissal for cause it is important to have complete evidence of the reasons for dismissal. This includes documentation and memoranda from supervisors and management.

o Where certain events are based on memory, the management personnel involved should be asked to prepare
detailed memoranda outlining all of the circumstances,
dates and other witnesses. This should be fully supported
by back-up documentation.

o Once documented, the dismissal should be carried out
promptly after the culminating incident. An unusual delay
could be seen to be as condonation or a waiver of the right
to dismiss for cause.

o All related documentation must be consistent with the dismissal for cause; that is, no severance pay should be paid.
Also, no letters of reference should be offered under the circumstances. Again, anything which is inconsistent with the
dismissal for cause could be seen to be a waiver of the
employer's right to dismiss for cause.

o If a severance offer is to be made, it should be in separate
correspondence on a "without prejudice" basis. That way, if
the severance is not accepted, the employer will be able to
rely on its right to dismiss for just cause.

o The employer must be prepared for an extensive legal battle. As the employee is fighting for his or her pride and
reputation, summary dismissal cases often go to trial.

o References regarding the former employee should not be
responded to. If management candidly outlines the reason
for termination of employment, the employee is very unlikely to get the job applied for. Then, if in subsequent legal
proceedings the court holds that the employer has not established cause, the period of unemployment is longer and
the employee may have an independent cause of action for
defamation. For similar reasons, letters of reference should
not be provided.

o If the employer wants to provide some response, simply
confirm the dates that the employee worked for the company, job title, and the nature of his or her duties.

o If asked to comment on the employee's performance or related questions, the employer can simply reply that its
policy is not to comment on the quality of an employee's
work.

3.7.2   DISMISSAL WITHOUT CAUSE

o Set a fair initial severance package or provide adequate advance notice of termination of employment.

o Employers may be reluctant to give working notice. They
may be concerned about a lack of productivity or a negative
impact on other employees. However, when coupled with a
generous severance package which is conditional upon
adequate and faithful performance, this can be an effective
means of getting productive work out of the employee.

o Some employers may prefer the salary and benefits continuance method; that is, the employee continues to receive
salary and benefits during the period of reasonable notice
but is relieved of the responsibilities to attend work. The advantage of this approach is that it can be structured so that
the salary and benefits end when the employee obtains
new employment. Then, as an added incentive the employee can also get a bonus representing 50% of the unpaid
salary. The disadvantage of this approach is that it makes it
difficult to tax shelter the money by rolling it into an
R.R.S.P., and the severance amount may actually be larger
because it is not as attractive to the employee as a lump
sum paid immediately following termination of employment.

o The employer should allow the employee at least seven
days to consider the offer, and should encourage the employee to obtain independent legal advice. This avoids a
later challenge to a settlement agreement or general
release where the employee attempts to argue that it was
signed under duress or without the benefit of legal advice.

o In the meantime, in order to avoid problems associated with
premature cancellation of benefits, the employee's benefits

can continue to run until the seven-day consideration period has expired.

o Where a large number of employees have been terminated at the same time, the employer should be careful not to allow negotiations of a larger severance package unless the initial offer was grossly unfair. If one employee is successful in negotiating for a larger severance package, other employees will usually find out and will want to have a larger severance package themselves. Of course, once a majority of the employees have accepted the packages and signed general releases, individual consideration can be given to any outstanding claims.

o Where a fair initial severance package has not been accepted, the employer may wish to invite the former employee to commence legal action and then defend against the claim. The defence would simply plead that reasonable notice had been provided (or reasonable compensation in lieu of notice), and therefore the claim should be dismissed.

o An offer of judgment can also be filed in court representing the severance package that the employer is prepared to offer. See: Chapter 7 – Negotiations and Settlement.

o The employer's counsel should resist going to trial until he or she has had a full opportunity to canvass the plaintiff's job search efforts and ascertain whether the former employee has mitigated damages by obtaining alternative employment during the period of reasonable notice.

o From time to time the employer will want to make casual enquiries within the industry to determine how the former employee's job search is going. Once alternative employment has been obtained, any outstanding offer should be reconsidered and revised in light of the new employment situation.

o The employer may wish to assist the former employee in securing alternative employment. This can include active searches and inquiries within the industry, together with positive recommendations on the employee's behalf.

o Once the plaintiff obtains other employment, this should enable the employer's counsel to make a precise calculation as to the amount of damages that would be recovered, and offer that as a settlement.

o If an offer of judgment has been served but not accepted, the plaintiff will be obligated to pay the employer's party and party costs in defending against the claim from the date the offer was served.

3.8 SPECIAL CASES

3.8.1 CONSTRUCTIVE DISMISSAL

o Where an employer makes a fundamental change in the duties of an employee, where there is a fundamental demotion, or where the duties are so significantly altered that they go to the very root of the employment contract, it may constitute a constructive dismissal. This does not include lateral transfers or a change in duties or reporting structure where it does not fundamentally alter the contract.

o A reduction in remuneration, or a change in the manner of compensation will constitute a constructive dismissal. However, where the benefits package is altered, the employee may have to remain in his or her employment and sue for damages. See *Hamilton & Olsen Surveys Ltd. v. Otto* (1993), 12 Alta. L.R. (3d) 431, (C.A.), leave to appeal to S.C.C. refused (1994), 15 Alta. L.R. (3d) lii (S.C.C.).

o In *Poulos v. Murphy Oil Co.* (1990), 75 Alta. L.R. (2d) 49 (Q.B.), the former manager of administration for the company faced corporate reorganization and a change of reporting structure. She lost her position on the management committee and was reporting to a vice president rather than to the president directly. The court dismissed her complaint of constructive dismissal and held that the reorganizational changes were not such as to go to the very root of the employment contract. This case suggests that Alberta employers have some latitude in reorganizing a corporation before it will amount to a constructive dismissal.

o In cases where there is a risk of a constructive dismissal arising, the employer should provide as much written notice as possible in advance of the change. If the employer can terminate employment upon reasonable notice, then unilateral changes can be made based on the same principle. Furthermore, if the employee continues to work after the changes have been implemented a court may hold that the employee has condoned the change.

o A change in the location of employment, if not bargained for at the beginning of employment, or if it is not implied because it is a customary practice in a particular business, will constitute a constructive dismissal.

o However, where an employee is part of a national or international corporation, it is often an implied term of the contract of employment that the employee will accept all reasonable regional transfers not involving a demotion or an undue burden or hardship. Where the employee accepts the transfer, he or she cannot later argue that this has amounted to a constructive dismissal.

o A supervisor's persistent criticisms of an employee's work without cause may also constitute a constructive dismissal, particularly where the employee is given no assistance in dealing with a superior or in relocating despite frequent requests for help. See: *Paitich v. Clarke Institute of Psychiatry* (1990), 30 C.C.E.L. 235 (Ont. C.A.).

o Some cases have held that when an employee has been constructively dismissed, he or she may be obligated to accept the changes to the terms and conditions of employment in order to mitigate damages. See: *Mifsud v. MacMillan Bathurst Inc.* (1989), 28 C.C.E.L. 228 (Ont. C.A.), leave to appeal to S.C.C. refused (1990), 68 D.L.R. (4th) vii (S.C.C.); *Hamilton & Olsen Surveys Ltd. v. Otto* (1993), 12 Alta. L.R. (3d) 431, (C.A.), leave to appeal to S.C.C. refused (1994), 15 Alta. L.R. (3d) lii (S.C.C.); but see: *Thiessen v. Leduc* (1975), [1975] 4 W.W.R. 387 (Alta. T.D.).

3.8.2   ILLNESS AND DISABILITY

o Illness or disability of a permanent nature will constitute a frustration of the employment contract. An illness or disability of a temporary nature will not amount to frustration. Therefore, employees who are off work due to a temporary illness or disability cannot be dismissed without notice.

o Furthermore, usually the period of reasonable notice cannot include the time during which the employee is off work due to illness or disability.

o Termination because of permanent illness or disability is based on the principle of frustration as opposed to the concept of just cause.

o Dismissal of an ill or disabled employee may also constitute discrimination on the ground of a physical or mental disability. This would be in violation of human rights legislation. It may also give rise to a duty of reasonable accommodation whereby the employer is obliged to find alternative employment for an employee who cannot perform his or her regular duties.

o Ill and disabled employees may also be entitled to short- and long-term disability benefits. Where these are wrongfully interfered with through a wrongful dismissal, the employer could be liable in damages.

o Therefore, prior to the termination of employees who are suffering from illness or disability, the employer must ensure that:

(i) The contract has been frustrated by an extended, or a very high rate of absence, and that it is very unlikely that the employee will be able to return to productive employment in the foreseeable future.

(ii) The medical standards are reasonable and constitute a *bona fide* occupational requirement.

(iii) The termination of employment does not interfere with short- or long-term disability benefits to which the employee is entitled.

   (iv) The employee is advised of all conversion privileges with respect to life insurance.

o For further information, see: D'Andrea, Corry and Forester, *Illness and Disability in the Workplace* (Canada Law Book, 1996).

3.8.3   EMPLOYEE DISHONESTY

o Employee dishonesty will justify dismissal for cause where the conduct seriously prejudices the employer's interest or reputation, or where the conduct reveals an untrustworthy character which undermines the position of responsibility or trust which is essential for the continued employment relationship.

o Mere suspicion of dishonesty and poor judgment on the part of the employee may not be sufficient to justify dismissal without notice.

o Employers must be very careful not to jump to premature conclusions in cases of employee dishonesty. The courts place a very heavy onus on an employer to prove dishonesty.

o The accusations of dishonesty have a severe, detrimental, and lasting impact on the employee. If the reasons for termination of the employment become known within the industry, it will be difficult if not impossible for the employee to obtain alternative employment.

o Where employers have improperly alleged dishonesty and have not proved it, the courts will often award punitive and aggravated damages and solicitor and client legal costs as a means of punishing the employer for it. See: *Francis v. Canadian Imperial Bank of Commerce* (1992), 41 C.C.E.L. 37 (Ont. Gen. Div.), reversed in part (1994), 7 C.C.E.L. (2d) 1 (C.A.).

o Where there is any uncertainty, the employer may wish to consider a temporary suspension of the employee pending completion of an investigation.

o In some cases, it may be appropriate to retain a private security firm to assist the employer in completing the investigation and in providing advice as to how to carry out the termination.

o In proven cases of dishonesty, the employer may wish to lay criminal charges and seek restitution through the criminal courts.

o Also, where there is a bond or insurance in place, the matter should be reported to the insurer.

3.8.4 SENIOR OFFICERS, DIRECTORS AND SHAREHOLDERS

o In some cases, senior officers, directors and shareholders are not employees. These individuals are not entitled to reasonable notice of termination or compensation in lieu of reasonable notice. See: *Re Leicester Club & Country Racecourse Co.* (1885), 30 Ch. D. 629.

o In cases where senior officers, directors and shareholders are also employees, the employer must consider whether their actions constitute oppression contrary to the Alberta *Business Corporations Act*, S.A. 1981, c. B-15.

o However, wrongful dismissal without more will not constitute oppression. See: *Welichka v. Bittner Investments Ltd.* (1988), 90 A.R. 224 (Q.B.); *Publow v. Wilson* (1995), 9 C.C.E.L. (2d) 30 (Ont. Gen. Div.).

o Where these persons are considered employees, they will also be entitled to damages for wrongful dismissal. See: *McGuire v. Wardair Canada Ltd.* (1969), 71 W.W.R. 705 (Alta. T.D.).

o In cases involving employees who are shareholders, careful consideration must be given to an offer to purchase the outstanding shares, as well as offering a fair severance package.

o A protracted and bitter dispute between senior officers, directors and shareholders of a company can often be very costly, time-consuming, emotionally draining, and detrimental to the company's business reputation.

3.8.5   HUMAN RIGHTS

o If the dismissal of the employee is a result of discrimination under one of the prohibited grounds, in addition to common law rights of wrongful dismissal, it may violate federal or provincial human rights legislation.

o o Under Alberta legislation, an employer is prohibited from discriminating against an employee on any of the following grounds: race, religious beliefs, colour, gender, physical disability, mental disability, age, ancestry, place of origin, family status or source of income. See: *Human Rights, Citizenship and Multiculturalism Act* ("*H.R.C.M.A.*"), R.S.A. 1980, c. H-11.7, s. 7.

o It is a complete defence if the employer can establish that the conduct is "reasonable and justifiable" in the circumstances or there is a *bona fide* occupational requirement (see: *HRCMA*, s. 7(3)). The employer may still have a duty to accommodate to the point of undue hardship however. See: *Central Alberta Dairy Pool v. Alberta (Human Rights Commission)* (1990), [1990] 2 S.C.R. 489.

o Employers under federal jurisdiction are subject to the *Canadian Human Rights Act* ("*C.H.R.A.*"), R.S.C. 1985, c. H-6, which prohibits discrimination on the following grounds: race, national or ethnic origin, colour, religion, age, sex, sexual orientation, marital status, family status, disability or conviction for an offence for which a pardon has been granted (see: s. 2, as amended).

o Again, if the employer can establish a *bona fide* occupational requirement, it is a complete defence. See: *C.H.R.A.*, s. 15.

o Any remedy under the human rights legislation is completely independent of common law rights and the human rights complaint may be filed and dealt with concurrently with the common law action for wrongful dismissal. Thus, the employer risks facing two concurrent actions if he or she dismisses the employee on the basis of a prohibited ground.

3.8.6 WRITTEN EMPLOYMENT CONTRACT

o Where an employee is dismissed without notice as provided for in an enforceable written agreement between the employer and the employee, or in accordance with the notice provisions set out in the contract, the employee is not entitled to damages in lieu of reasonable notice. See: *Toronto-Dominion Bank v. Wallace* (1983), 41 O.R. (2d) 161 (C.A.); *Pierce v. Krahn* (1979), 10 Alta. (2d) 49 (T.D.).

o The stipulated notice period in a personnel manual, however, is not a contract and will not deprive employees of their common law right to notice.

o If the contract of employment provides that employment can be terminated at any time by either party, with or without cause, the employee is still entitled to reasonable notice where the contract does not provide for termination without notice.

o Where the employment contract is for a fixed term, and the employment is terminated at the end of term, the employee is not entitled to any notice or pay in lieu.

o Where an employment contract circumvents the common law rights of the employee, the contract may be unenforceable on a number of grounds:

(i) If the contract is harsh or unconscionable, was signed under duress or is so unreasonable as to amount to a penalty. This argument could apply to an unreasonably low notice provision or an unreasonably high one.

119

(ii) Where the contract provides for termination upon less notice than the minimum standards set out in the *Employment Standards Act, supra.* In that case the employee is entitled to his or her full common law rights. See: *Machtinger v. HOJ Industries Ltd.*, [1992] 1 S.C.R. 986.

(iii) The terms and conditions in the standard form contract have not been actually agreed to, do not cover the whole agreement of the parties, or are inappropriate in the context of the job.

(iv) The contract was drawn up at the time of hiring into a specified position, and the employee has assumed duties beyond the scope of those referred to in the contract (e.g., promotion or transfer).

(v) The employer offered the job and it was accepted by the employee before tendering the formal written contract.

3.8.7   INDEPENDENT CONTRACTOR

o The court will look at all of the circumstances of the case to determine the true relationship as to whether it is that of an independent contractor or an employee. See: Section 1.2.2, *supra.*

o An independent contractor is generally not entitled to damages for wrongful dismissal. However, if the contract is one of an indefinite duration, the independent contractor may be entitled to reasonable notice of termination, except for termination for just cause.

o Although an independent contractor is not entitled to the minimum employment standards set out in the *E.S.C.*, employers must be careful to ensure that an agreement has been reached as to the duration of the contract or the period of reasonable notice that either party must give to the other to terminate the relationship.

3.9 RELATED CLAIMS

3.9.1 EMPLOYMENT STANDARDS

o The employment standards legislation sets out the minimum period of notice and does not affect the requisite period of notice as determined by common law.

o The *E.S.C.* also prescribes legislative standards with respect to the payment of wages, overtime, general holidays, vacation pay and other entitlements.

o An employee who has been dismissed may also have certain claims under the *E.S.C.*. These claims are initiated by a complaint to an Employment Standards Officer, followed by an investigation, and an attempt to resolve the claim.

o Valid claims that have not been resolved will be the subject of an order of the Employment Standards Officer.

o If not complied with, the order is enforceable upon registration with the Court of Queen's Bench. Appeals may be made to an umpire (usually a small claims judge).

3.9.2 HUMAN RIGHTS

o Where an employee is dismissed on any of the following grounds, it may constitute discrimination contrary to the human rights legislation: race, religious beliefs, colour, gender, physical disability, mental disability, marital status, age, criminal conviction with pardon granted, ancestry, place of origin, family status or source of income. See: *H.R.C.M.A.*, s. 7, and *C.H.R.A.*, s. 2.

o In those cases, employers could be faced with both a common law action for wrongful dismissal and a human rights complaint under the statutory scheme.

3.9.3   DISABILITY BENEFITS

o A wrongfully-dismissed employee who is totally disabled may have a claim for disability benefits under the short- or long-term disability plan.

o Where the employee's eligibility for disability benefits has been taken away because of insufficient notice of dismissal, the employer may be directly liable for those benefits. Employers will therefore want to ensure that disability coverage will not be affected by the termination of employment.

o In cases where the employee becomes disabled following termination of employment, the employer may wish to reinstate disability benefits until it is clear that the employee will not be advancing a claim.

3.9.4   MISREPRESENTATION

o An employee may have a related cause of action for negligent or intentional misrepresentation. See: *Queen v. Cognos Inc.* (1993), [1993] 1 S.C.R. 87.

o An employer may be able to avoid exposure to an action for negligent misrepresentation by making it clear in the offer of employment that the employee is only relying on the written offer and not on any oral representations.

o In defending a misrepresentation law suit, the employer must have clear and unequivocal evidence as to exactly what was stated during the hiring process and show that all of the representations were true. Alternatively, the employer may defend against the action by showing that the employee did not rely on the representations or has not incurred any damages as a result.

122

3.9.5 HARASSMENT

o There is no common law right of action for harassment *per se*. However, where harassment by a supervisor constitutes intentional infliction of mental suffering, the employer may be vicariously liable. See: *Boothman v. R.* (1993), 49 C.C.E.L. 109 (Fed. T.D.).

o In order to defend against an action for harassment, the employer should be encouraged to adopt and enforce an anti-harassment policy.

o This policy should encourage all supervisors to act professionally in their dealings with their employees. If there are any incidents of harassment, there should be a means of communicating this to senior management on a confidential basis. Any complaints of harassment should be dealt with promptly and fairly.

o In defending against an action for harassment, the employer can indicate that it exercised all due diligence to avoid harassment and that the senior employee acted beyond the scope of his duties in perpetrating the harassment of the employee.

3.9.6 WORKERS' COMPENSATION

o An employee who has sustained an industrial accident will be entitled to claim for Workers' Compensation benefits.

o Dismissal from employment will not affect the employee's entitlement to Workers' Compensation.

o The accident will be charged to the former employer, and this will likely increase the employer's assessment based on its experience rating.

o Where the worker is unemployed, the period of rehabilitation is usually longer because there is less incentive to return to work.

3.9.7   DEFAMATION AND REFERENCE CHECKS

o Where an employer makes defamatory remarks or publishes a defamatory statement about a former employee it may give rise to a related cause of action in defamation. A claim in defamation may be combined with a claim of wrongful dismissal. If established, it could result in general damages, aggravated or punitive damages, and possibly solicitor and client legal costs. See: *Francis v. Canadian Imperial Bank of Commerce* (1992), 41 C.C.E.L. 37, (Ont. Gen. Div.), reversed in part (1994), 7 C.C.E.L. (2d) 1 (C.A.); *Domtar Inc. c. St-Germain* (1991), 38 C.C.E.L. 267 (C.A.).

o Employers must be careful to avoid making any defamatory or libellous remarks in providing letters of reference or in response to reference checks.

o Where there is any doubt, a prudent policy is simply to provide the dates of employment, the nature of the job and the duties performed. If the inquirer asks any questions related to job performance, simply state that it is the policy of the company not to comment on performance or provide any indication as to whether the employee would be re-hired or not.

3.9.8   LABOUR BOARD

o Where a dismissal, in whole or in part, results from union activity or the employee's support for a trade union, it constitutes an unfair labour practice contrary to the Alberta *Labour Relations Code*, S.A. 1988, c. L-1.2, or the *Canada Labour Code* ("*C.L.C.*"), R.S.C. 1985, c. L-2.

o A former employee who feels that he or she has been dismissed as a result of union activity or choice of a labour union, may complain to the Labour Board. If the complaint is established, one of the remedies available to the Board is reinstatement.

o This does not preclude an employer from dismissing an employee for just cause. However, once the former employee establishes that the employer is aware of union activity, the onus shifts to the employer to establish that the union activity had nothing to do with the dismissal. Therefore, such cases must be carefully documented.

3.9.9   UNSAFE WORK

o Under occupational health and safety legislation, an employee has the right to refuse unsafe work. See: Alberta *Occupational Health and Safety Act,* R.S.A. 1980, c. O-2, ss. 27 and 28; *C.L.C.* (Part II), s. 128.

o If an employee is fired because of his or her refusal to perform unsafe work, he or she may complain to an occupational health and safety officer who will investigate the matter and order reinstatement where appropriate.

o In defending against such claims, the employer must establish that the work was safe and that there was no objective basis for the employee's concerns about safety.

3.10   CLAIMS AGAINST EMPLOYEES

o Employers may have claims against their former employees which may properly be the subject of an independent cause of action or a counterclaim against an employee who has sued for wrongful dismissal.

3.10.1   DISHONESTY

o In cases of theft, fraud or other dishonesty, an employer may bring a claim for its loss against the former employee. This may include a restitution claim through the criminal process or a civil action.

o Where an insurance or bonding company is involved, one of the conditions of insurance coverage may mandate that criminal charges be laid and that a subrogated action be commenced by the employer on behalf of the insurance company to recover the loss.

3.10.2   BREACH OF DUTY TO THE EMPLOYER

o All employees have a duty of fidelity to their employer. This prevents the employee from personally profiting through the employer's business and from unfairly competing with the employer during the tenure of employment.

o If an employee diverts business away from the employer for personal profit, whether this arises directly or indirectly, it is a breach of the duty of fidelity.

o Similarly, if the employee solicits business from the employer's customers and clients, it is a breach of the duty of fidelity.

o Officers, directors and senior employees have a broader fiduciary duty, in addition to the duty of fidelity. As a fiduciary, the senior employee must always act with the utmost good faith and in the best interests of the employer. Generally this means that he or she cannot compete directly with the employer, both during employment and for a reasonable period of time following termination of the employment.

o This prevents the senior employee from taking advantage of any incipient business opportunity, and competing unfairly against the former employer following termination of employment. See: *Tree Savers International Ltd. v. Savoy* (1991), 81 Alta. L.R. (2d) 325 (Q.B.), varied (1992), 84 Alta. L.R. (2d) 384 (C.A.).

o An employer who has incurred damages as a result of a breach of the fiduciary duty or the duty of fidelity may bring a claim against the former employee.

o Furthermore, where the employer suffers irreparable harm as a result of unfair competition from a former employee who was in a fiduciary capacity, the employer may be able

126

to get an interim injunction restraining the unfair competition pending trial.

3.10.3   NEGLIGENCE

o Where an employee has been negligent, the employer may have an independent cause of action to recover its loss which has resulted from the employee's negligent activities.

o Such actions are rare because if the negligence occurred in the normal and usual performance of the employee's duties, the courts imply that the employer will indemnify the employee for such actions.

o However, in clear cases of negligence where the employee has clearly neglected his or her duties, or has committed a negligent act outside of the scope of normal duties, it may justify a negligence action to recover damages. See: *Dominion Manufacturers Ltd. v. O'Gorman* (1989), 24 C.C.E.L. 218 (Ont. Dist. Ct.); *Overmyer Co. of Canada Ltd. v. Wallace Transfer Ltd.* (1975), 65 D.L.R. (3d) 717 (B.C.C.A.).

3.10.4   RESTRICTIVE COVENANTS

o Some cases arise where employees have signed restrictive covenants upon hiring or as a condition of continued employment. These agreements purport to prevent the employee from competing against the employer during the term of employment and for a given period following termination of employment.

o As these are covenants in restraint of trade, they are narrowly enforced by the courts only under the following circumstances:
   o Where it is reasonable for the employer to have a restrictive covenant.
   o Where the duration of the covenant is reasonable.
   o Where the geographical scope of the covenant is reasonable; that is, it only applies to the area where the

employer is carrying on business and is only broad enough to protect the employer's customer base at the time of termination of employment.

o An employer may sue for damages or obtain an injunction against an employee who has violated an enforceable restrictive covenant.

o However, on public policy grounds, if the court holds that the restrictive covenant is unreasonable or onerous, it will be struck down.

3.10.5   OTHER DAMAGES

o Other actions by employees may give rise to a damages claim, such as violation of the employer's intellectual property rights, defamatory statements which effect the employer's reputation, etc.

3.11   DEFENCE OF THE CLAIM

3.11.1   RETAINER AND NOTIFICATION OF OPPOSING COUNSEL

o The employer will either be notified of the claim through discussions with the former employee or their legal counsel.

o Once retained, notify the opposing counsel by telephone and advise that you have been retained. Ask that all further discussions take place among legal counsel, and request that no further steps be taken without reasonable notification to your office.

o If a statement of claim has been filed, protect the employer's interest by obtaining an indulgence or extension from the plaintiff's counsel for filing the defence, preferably in writing.

o If the statement of claim has not been filed, obtain instruction from the employer to admit the service of the statement of claim and provide an undertaking to file a statement of defence in due course.

3.11.2 STATEMENT OF DEFENCE

o The purpose of the statement of defence in a wrongful dismissal action is to outline the basic facts relied upon by the employer in defence of the claim. The employer should readily admit those facts which are not in dispute, and only put in issue those facts which are.

o The following general issues may be in dispute in a wrongful dismissal claim:

  o Whether the plaintiff is an employee of the defending employer? (i.e., he or she may be an employee of another party, an independent contractor, an agent, a volunteer, etc.).
  o Whether there was just cause for termination.
  o Whether there was notice of termination and whether reasonable notice or severance pay has been provided.
  o Whether any damages are sought in counterclaim.

o If the employment relationship is in issue, the statement of defence should deny that the plaintiff is an employee and set out the true relationship of the plaintiff.

o If the employment relationship is admitted, correct any facts which are not properly pleaded.

o If the employee was dismissed for cause, plead that fact and briefly set out the grounds.

o If the employee was not dismissed for cause, plead that the employee was provided with reasonable notice or compensation in lieu of notice. Set out the period of notice provided to the employee and any severance amounts paid.

o Deny any liability for other claims such as mental suffering, punitive or aggravated damages, etc.

o Plead that the plaintiff has failed to mitigate damages.

o In the alternative, plead that the damages claimed by the plaintiff under the circumstances are excessive.

o See generally: Appendix 3D – Sample Statement of Defence.

3.12   COUNTERCLAIM

o If the employer wishes to advance a claim against a former employee, this should be set out in a counterclaim, which should be joined in the statement of defence.

o The counterclaim must set out all of the material facts upon which the employer relies and establish an independent cause of action.

o The client should be advised that the counterclaim could add to the cost and complexity of the litigation. If such a claim is not established, the client could be liable for the costs of the plaintiff in defending against the counterclaim.

3.13   ACTION

o Prepare a "to do" check list which may include the following items.

3.13.1   THE LAWYER'S "TO DO" CHECK LIST

o Phone opposing counsel advising that you represent client and ask that all further communications be through your office.
o If a statement of claim has been filed, ask for time to file the defence. If not served, advise that you will accept service and will undertake to defend.
o Obtain a copy of correspondence from the opposing counsel. Order the statement of claim and the entire personnel file.

o Interview potential management witnesses, and have them prepare memoranda.
o Research any issues as to cause.
o Evaluate the range of reasonable notice and damages.
o Respond to the opposing counsel.
o Prepare draft statement of defence and review it with the client.
o Once finalized, file and serve the statement of defence.

3.13.2   THE CLIENT'S "TO DO" CHECK LIST

o Provide copies of the Record of Employment, personnel file, applicable policies, benefit booklets, and other relevant documents.
o If the employee has signed an employment contract, confidentiality and non-competition covenant, or other similar documents, provide copies.
o Provide copies of any employment appraisals, letters of warning, or memoranda pertaining to other disciplinary action.
o Provide detailed memoranda of the circumstances leading to termination of employment.
o Obtain information and memoranda from supervisors regarding the former employee's performance.
o Consider whether there is any basis for a counterclaim and provide copies of relevant documents.
o Review the draft statement of defence and provide comments to legal counsel.
o Make inquiries regarding alternative employment in the industry that would be suited to the former employee.
o Through informal contacts, find out if the plaintiff obtained alternative employment.

APPENDIX 3A
Client Interview Checklist

Wrongful Dismissal Claim – Employer

Name of Client:

Client's Address:

Contact Person/Title:

Phone:

Telefax:

E-mail Address:

Details on Employee Dismissed

Name:

Title:

Age:

Date Commenced Employment:

Date of Dismissal:

Date Notice Given:

Amount of Severance Paid:

Range of Reasonable Notice:

Range of Damages:

Employment History

Job Title	Age	Dates	Place	Reporting To	Salary

Hiring and Interview for the Job

Advertisement or posting   ☐ Yes   ☐ No

How found out about the job?

Unemployed at the time?

Who interviewed? Any representations made?   ☐ Yes   ☐ No

     Details: _____

_____

_____

_____

_____

Letter of hire?   ☐ Yes   ☐ No

Sign any documents?   ☐ Yes   ☐ No

Employment contract   ☐ Yes   ☐ No

Confidentiality/Non-competition covenant   ☐ Yes   ☐ No

Agreements   ☐ Yes   ☐ No

Other documents? _____

_____

- Member of Union?   ☐ Yes   ☐ No

  - Collective agreement   ☐ Yes   ☐ No

- Review résumé or employment and educational background for each employee.

- Age of each employee

- Review performance for each employee:

  - Evaluations?

  - Warnings?

  - Discipline?

  - How well did employee get along with others?
    - Supervisors
    - Colleagues

- Circumstances leading to termination?

_____

_____

_____

- Reasons for Termination?

_____

_____

_____

- Is cause in issue? ☐ Yes ☐ No

Damages Evaluation

- Salary/wages: $ _____

- Other remuneration?

- Bonuses: ☐ Discretionary ☐ Non-discretionary

- Details:
  - Overtime
  - Commissions
  - Other

134

- Incentive Plans?

• Stock options	□ Yes	□ No
• Savings plans	□ Yes	□ No
• Stock purchase plans	□ Yes	□ No
• Others	□ Yes	□ No

- Retirement Plans?

• Pension	□ Yes	□ No
• Defined benefit plan	□ Yes	□ No
• Defined contribution plan	□ Yes	□ No
• Individual pension plan	□ Yes	□ No
• Group R.R.S.P.	□ Yes	□ No
• Other	□ Yes	□ No

BENEFITS	YES	NO	EMPLOYEE PAYS	EMPLOYER PAYS
Short-term Illness/Disability				
Long-term Disability				
Life Insurance • Basic • Additional Amount _____ • Conversion Options □ Yes □ No _____ days				
Accidental Death & Dismemberment				
Alberta Health Care □ Family □ Single				
Extended Health				
Dental				

Automobile/Travel Benefit _____

_____

_____

Other benefits:

Vacation

- Annual vacation entitlement _____ weeks.

- Any accrued or unused vacation   ☐   Yes   ☐   No

  amount _____

- Vacation pay paid?   ☐ Yes   ☐ No   Amount: $ _____

Illness/Disability Issues

- Was the employee ill or disabled at the time of termination?

- On Workers' Compensation? Since when?

- On L.T.D.? Since when?

- Unemployment Insurance benefits?
  - Has a Record of Employment been issued? ☐ Yes ☐ No
  - What is the reason for termination on the Record of Employment? ____
  - Is there an issue as to entitlement for unemployment benefits? ☐ Yes ☐ No
  - Has there been any correspondence or communications with the commission? ☐ Yes ☐ No
    - Review.

Pension/Retirement Issues

- Are any employees eligible to retire soon?

- Is the pension vested?   ☐   Yes   ☐   No

- Type of pension? _____

- Is there an opportunity to enhance the pension plan? ☐ Yes ☐ No

  - Review with actuary.

Final Paycheque

- All wages/salary and other remuneration paid to date? ☐ Yes ☐ No

- Vacation pay?   Amount? $ _____

- Any pay in lieu of notice? Amount? $ _____

Letters of Reference

- Any letters of reference provided?

- What is the employer's policy in providing letters of reference?

Other Claims

- Any Employment Standards claims or issues?   ☐ Yes   ☐ No

- Any Human Rights claims or issues?   ☐ Yes   ☐ No

- Have any settlement discussions been held?   ☐ Yes   ☐ No

- Has outplacement counselling been offered?   ☐ Yes   ☐ No

  - Firm: _____

  - Details: _____

    _____

    _____

Past History

- Has the employer dismissed any employees in the recent past?

- Brief history of those cases.

_____

_____

- Was a specific severance formula offered?

- Were settlements reached with the other employees?

- Would any of these employees be potential adverse witnesses?

APPENDIX 3B

Letter Confirming Retainer

Lawyer's Name
Direct Line:
Our File No.:

*Date

*Address

Dear Sir/Madame:

Re: *

We wish to thank you for retaining our firm to act on your behalf in regard to the above action. We are writing to confirm that we are prepared to act on your behalf and to outline the terms of our understanding.

Following our initial consultation on *, you instructed us to examine the demand letter from your former employee and recommend whether the requested amount of compensation stated therein is acceptable in lieu of reasonable notice of termination. If the settlement offer is not agreed to by the expiry date set out in that letter, then the Plaintiff will likely issue a Statement of Claim against [You/Your Company] commencing litigation in the Alberta Court of Queen's Bench.

Once the Statement of Claim has been served on you, you will be required to file a Statement of Defence. The Court allows 15 days from the date of service of the Statement of Claim for you to prepare and file a Statement of Defence. However, this deadline is commonly extended as a courtesy as between counsel to enable an employer sufficient time to retain a lawyer and to prepare a Statement of Defence. It is possible however that counsel for the Plaintiff may be instructed by your former employee to not grant any extension to you in this action, but this occurs in only rare cases where such instruction has been made clear to us.

Once all of the pleadings have been filed and closed, then Examinations for Discovery will be held whereby we will be given an opportunity to examine the Plaintiff and their counsel will be given an opportunity to examine you. Upon completion of the Examinations for Discovery and all other interlocutory matters, the action will then be set down for trial.

It is anticipated that most of the work with respect to this litigation will be performed by the writer, however, other lawyers in our firm may be utilized to perform legal services where, in our judgment, such assistance is necessary or desirable, particularly where a more junior lawyer can perform services in a more cost-effective manner.

Our fees will be based principally on the time spent by us on your behalf, although we reserve the right to adjust our rates in appropriate circumstances, such as where exceptionally efficient representation is made, or where circumstances are pressing or where special demands may be made of us. We also confirm that the writer's current hourly rate is $* per hour, which is subject to be increased from time to time, and is reviewed on an annual basis in [Month]. We also advise that the amount charged per hour increases with the experience and seniority of the lawyer conducting work on your behalf and if more senior counsel are involved, the hourly rate can be higher than that of the writer.

You will also be responsible for reimbursing us for disbursements and other charges incurred on your behalf. Such disbursements and other charges may include expenses such as telephone calls, postage, deliveries, photocopying, telecopies, court fees, word processing, and other reasonable out-of-pocket expenses.

At this stage, we cannot accurately assess what our legal fees might be, and this is particularly difficult when you are involved in litigation. Although the majority of cases settle prior to trial, the acceptance or rejection of a settlement depends ultimately on whether your former employee offers a settlement which is acceptable to you or whether [He/She] accepts our counteroffer. If the settlement is not agreed to, then the Plaintiff will likely proceed with the litigation and ultimately to trial. The amount of the total legal fees involved will depend largely on the steps taken in this action.

We shall require an initial retainer of $*, which will serve as a source of payment of our interim accounts when rendered. We also confirm that you will be providing us with a series of post-dated cheques in the amount of $* to be deposited each month as a retainer toward future legal fees. Any unused portion of the retainer will be returned to you upon completion of our services, and as the retainer is used from time to time a further retainer may be requested.

Interim accounts will be rendered on a regular basis, and will detail the services performed, the legal fees charged, and the disbursements incurred. A final account will be rendered at the conclusion of the action, taking into consideration a number of factors. If you have any questions concerning our accounts, please feel free to discuss it with us. If you feel that the fee charged is unfair, you have a right to have the account taxed before a Taxing Officer of the Court of Queen's Bench. In regard to lawyer's fees, you may wish to refer to the enclosed brochure which is published by the Law Society of Alberta.

Accounts must be paid within * days of receipt. If any account remains overdue, the firm has the right to cease all further work until full payment has been made, and may cease to act on your behalf should that be necessary. In addition, legal proceedings may be taken in order to collect the outstanding account.

As we advised you during our initial meeting on *, in our view, some courts do not view dismissal due to economic circumstances or corporate reorganization as just cause at Common Law. Furthermore, while the severance pay offered to your former employee in the sum of $* constitutes an appropriate amount under the *Employment Standards Code* of Alberta, [He/She] may be entitled to a longer period of notice or pay in lieu of notice under the Common Law.

That being said, the Plaintiff is also under a duty to seek alternative employment as diligently as possible. If [He/She] does not actively seeking alternative employment, [His/Her] damages award could ultimately be reduced for "failure to mitigate [His/Her] damages". Furthermore, once the Plaintiff obtains alternative employment, the amount that [He/She] earns in [His/Her] new job may reduce the damages award to which [He/She] are otherwise entitled at Common Law.

Given the expense of wrongful dismissal litigation to former employees, it is likely that the Plaintiff will be highly motivated to accept a settlement offer as early as possible in the process. Of course, there are a number of advantages to a speedy settlement to you as well. With this in mind, I will examine the demand letter and provide you with my recommendations as soon as possible.

We are appreciative of this opportunity to be of service to you. Should you have any questions or concerns regarding these arrangements, the service provided by us, or our advice to date, we would be pleased to discuss this with you.

Yours very truly,

LAW FIRM NAME

[Your Name]

APPENDIX 3C

Severance Packages

1. Reasonable Notice

[EMPLOYER LETTERHEAD]

* Date

DELIVERED BY HAND

PERSONAL & CONFIDENTIAL

* Employee's Name and Address

Dear *:

As discussed in our meeting today, I regret to inform you that your employment is terminated effective [Date]. This decision has been made after very careful consideration and is irrevocable. Your position has been eliminated due to a restructuring which requires an individual with engineering qualifications. You are relieved of your job responsibilities immediately in order that you may pursue other career opportunities.

Your regular pay for the period ending [Date] will be deposited in your bank account. Provided that it is acceptable to your benefits carriers, your group benefits including Alberta Health Care, group life insurance, extended health care, dental care, and disability insurance will be continued until [Date], or until you obtain employment, whichever comes first. Within thirty (30) days of discontinuance of your group life insurance coverage, you have the option to convert that coverage to private insurance. Further details regarding this option are available by contacting the following individual:

> [Name of Insurance contact or person within the company that can be contacted]

In addition to your regular salary and benefits, you are entitled to * days vacation pay in the sum of $_____. This amount will be included in your final pay at the end of the month.

Your Stock Option Agreement will be delivered to you as soon as it is available.

We confirm that you currently have an option pertaining to * shares in [Employer Name] at the option price of $* per share. Although given the share price it is highly unlikely that you will want to exercise your option, however if you wish to do so, you have ninety (90) days to exercise the option after termination of your employment. Except in the event of a change of control within ninety (90) days, which is not expected, no further shares will vest to you under the option plan.

Attached is a "without prejudice" severance offer to pay you in lieu of reasonable notice of termination of employment based on your service with the company as an employee. Please carefully consider this offer and advise us as to your response on or before the close of business on [Date]. If the offer is unacceptable, you will receive only those amounts to which you are entitled under the *Employment Standards Code*.

I sincerely thank you for your past service to [Employer] and wish you every success in your future endeavors.

Yours truly,

[Name of Employer's Officer]

[Executive Position of Officer]

2. Pay in Lieu of Reasonable Notice

[EMPLOYER LETTERHEAD]

[Date]

DELIVERED BY HAND

PERSONAL & CONFIDENTIAL

"WITHOUT PREJUDICE"

[Employee's Name and Address]

Dear *:

Further to my letter of [Date] advising you of the termination of your employment, I am pleased to offer the following severance package in recognition of your service to [Employer] and to assist you in transition while you seek suitable alternative employment. This severance package is offered on a completely "without prejudice" basis, in full and final settlement of any claims against [Employer], and is subject to the terms and conditions outlined below:

1. [Employer] will pay a lump-sum severance amount in the sum of $*, less all statutory deductions, representing * months salary.

2. You may elect to roll all or a portion of your severance pay into an R.R.S.P., pursuant to the *Income Tax Act*, in which case tax will not be withheld on the applicable amount. In that case, you must provide us with a duly executed Revenue Canada TD2 Form. These forms are available from a financial institution where you have your R.R.S.P.

3. Payment of your severance package will be conditional upon your execution of the enclosed General Release, the terms of which are expressly made part of this offer of settlement. The severance and benefits payments will be paid within a reasonable period of time following your acceptance of the offer.

This offer is open for acceptance until [Time], [Date], failing which it will be automatically withdrawn. If it is acceptable, please deliver one copy of the enclosed General Release to me by the above deadline. If this offer is not accepted by that date, you will be paid only those amounts to which you are entitled under the *Employment Standards Code*. We recommend that you obtain independent legal advice pertaining to this offer. I look forward to your response.

Yours truly,

[Name of Employer's Officer]
[Executive Position of Officer]

enclosure (General Release)

3. General Release

1. RELEASE

IN CONSIDERATION of payment to me by [Employer] in the amount of [Severance Amount] Dollars ($*), less sums required by law to be withheld, receipt of which is hereby acknowledged, I, [Employee's Name], do for myself and my heirs, executors, administrators and assigns, (hereinafter collectively referred to as "I"), forever release, remise and discharge [Employer], its subsidiaries and affiliates and all its officers, directors, employees, agents, insurers and assigns (hereinafter collectively referred to as the "Company"), jointly and severally from any and all actions, causes of actions, contracts, (whether express or implied), claims and demands for damages, loss, or injury, suits, debts, sums of money, indemnity, expenses, interest, costs and claims of any and every kind and nature whatsoever, at law or in equity, which against the Company, I ever had, now have, or can hereafter have by reasons of or existing out of any causes whatsoever existing up to and inclusive of the date of this Release, including but without limiting the generality of the foregoing:

(a) my employment with the Company;

(b) the termination of my employment with the Company; and

(c) any and all claims for damages, salary, wages, termination pay, severance pay, vacation pay, commissions, bonuses, expenses, allowances, incentive payments, insurance or any other benefits arising out of my employment with the Company.

2. NO ADMISSION

I acknowledge that the payment given to me pursuant to the above paragraph does not constitute any admission of liability by or on behalf of the Company.

3. INDEMNITY FOR TAXES, ETC.

I further agree that, for the aforesaid payment, I will save harmless and indemnify the Company from and against all claims, taxes or penalties and demands, which may be made by the Minister of National Revenue requiring the Company to pay income tax under the *Income Tax Act* (Canada) in respect of income tax payable by myself in excess of the income tax previously withheld; and in respect of any and all claims, charges, taxes, or penalties and demands which may be made on behalf of or related to the Canada Employment and Immigration Commission or the Canada Pension Commission under the applicable statutes and regulations, with respect to any amount which may, in the future, be found to be payable by the Company in respect of myself.

4. EMPLOYMENT STANDARDS

I acknowledge receipt of all wages, overtime pay, vacation pay, general holiday pay, and pay in place of termination of employment that I am entitled to by virtue of the *Employment Standards Code* or pursuant to any other labour standards legislation and I further confirm that there are no entitlements, overtime pay or wages due and owing to myself by the Company.

5. BENEFITS AND INSURANCE CLAIMS

I acknowledge and agree that the payment to me includes full compensation and consideration for loss of employment benefits and that all of my employment benefits have ceased on [Date]. I acknowledge that I have received all benefit entitlements, including insurance benefits to date, and have no further claim against the Company for benefits. I fully accept sole responsibility to replace those benefits that I wish to continue and to exercise conversion privileges where applicable with respect to benefits. In the event that I become disabled after [Date], I covenant not to sue the Company for insurance or other benefits, or for loss of benefits. I hereby release the Company from any further obligations or liabilities arising from my employment benefits after [Date].

6. NON-DISCLOSURE

I agree that I will not divulge or disclose, directly or indirectly, the contents of this Release or the terms of settlement relating to the termination of my employment with the company to any person, including but without limiting the generality of the foregoing, to employees or former employees of the company, except my legal and financial advisors on the condition that they maintain the confidentiality thereof, or as required by law.

7. CONFIDENTIALITY

I recognize and acknowledge that during my employment with the Company I had access to certain confidential and proprietary information, the disclosure of which could be harmful to the interests of the Company. I acknowledge and agree that I have taken and will in future take appropriate precautions to safeguard the Confidential Information of the Company. Further, I agree that I will respect and abide by any Employee Confidentiality of Assignment of Rights Agreements that I have executed.

8. FURTHER CLAIMS

I agree not to make claim or take proceedings against any other person or corporation that might claim contribution or indemnity under the provisions of any statute or otherwise against the Company.

9. UNDERSTANDING

AND I HEREBY DECLARE that I have had the opportunity to seek independent legal advice with respect to the matters addressed in this Release and the terms of settlement which have been agreed to by myself and the Company and that I fully understand this Release and the terms of settlement. I have not been influenced by any representations or statements made by or on behalf of the Company. I hereby voluntarily accept the said terms for the purpose of making full and final compromise, adjustment and settlement of all claims as aforesaid.

10. COMPLETE AGREEMENT

I understand and agree that this Release contains the entire agreement between the Company and me and that the terms of this Release are contractual and not a mere recital.

DATED at the City of *, in the Province of Alberta, this * day of [Month], 199*.

_____   _____
WITNESS   [EMPLOYEE NAME]

APPENDIX 3D

Sample Statement of Defence

IN THE COURT OF QUEEN'S BENCH OF ALBERTA
JUDICIAL CENTRE OF *

BETWEEN:

*

Plaintiff

- and -

*

Defendant

STATEMENT OF DEFENCE

1. The Defendant admits the allegations in paragraphs * and * of the Statement of Claim. The Defendant denies all other allegations contained in the Statement of Claim.

2. The Defendant denies that the Plaintiff was wrongfully dismissed from [His/Her] employment as alleged and states that the Plaintiff's employment was terminated for just cause on or about [Date] on the grounds of insubordination, misconduct and incompetence in the performance of [His/Her] job as [Position], particulars of which are as follows:

(a) [He/She] failed to devote [His/Her] efforts to the performance of [His/Her] job during working hours and spent a great deal of time conducting personal business during working hours;

(b) [He/She] was excessively slow in the performance of [His/Her] job;

(c) [He/She] totally ignored important deadlines and on some occasions completely abandoned tasks which were assigned;

(d) [He/She] went on holidays without informing [His/Her] immediate superiors, and took more than [His/Her] holiday entitlement within a holiday year; and

(e) [He/She] displayed a poor attitude toward [His/Her] immediate superiors thereby creating an atmosphere in the office of employment which adversely affected the supervision and delegation of tasks.

[Other Particulars, If Applicable]

3. As a result of the Plaintiff's insubordination, misconduct and incompetence, the Defendant sustained excessive financial loss and was compelled to delegate numerous projects which had been assigned to the Plaintiff to other employees, who worked long hours under pressure in order to perform the re-assigned tasks.

4. The Defendant had repeatedly warned the Plaintiff that [His/Her] job performance was unacceptable and frequent meetings were held with the Plaintiff in order to outline the Defendant's concerns, stipulate the standard expected and to assist the Plaintiff in the performance of [His/Her] job. In spite of these meetings, which were held intermittently over the course of approximately one year prior to the termination of the Plaintiff's employment, the Plaintiff's job performance did not improve.

5. The Defendant therefore denies that the Plaintiff is entitled to reasonable notice of dismissal, and further denies that the Plaintiff has suffered any damages for which the Defendant is, in law, liable.

6. In the further alternative, the Defendant states that the Plaintiff has failed to mitigate [His/Her] damages.

WHEREFORE THE DEFENDANT PRAYS THAT THE PLAINTIFF'S CLAIM BE DISMISSED WITH COSTS.

DATED at the [City/Town] of [Place], in the Province of Alberta this [Date] AND DELIVERED by [Name of Firm], Barristers and Solicitors, solicitors for the within Defendant, whose address for service is in care of the said solicitors at [Address].

APPENDIX 3E

Wrongful Dismissal Litigation Timeline – Defendant

ACTING FOR THE DEFENDANT

1. Forward letter to opposing counsel advising that we have been retained to act and request that reasonable notice be provided prior to any further steps.

2. Conduct corporate search of parties.

3. Arrange for initial meeting with clients.

4. Prepare draft Statement of Defence.

5. Forward draft Statement of Defence for client's review and comments.

6. File and serve Statement of Defence together with Demand for Discovery and Notice to Produce.

7. Prepare draft Affidavit of Documents and Production.

    (a) Letter to client re producible documents;

    (b) Photocopy and organize producible documents Copies: client, other side, working copies; and

    (c) Original documents to be retained in separate folio.

8. Send standard letter enclosing draft Affidavit and producible documents to other counsel (cc. client).

9. Request other parties draft Affidavit and copies of producible documents.

10. Schedule Examinations for Discovery:

    (a) Phone other parties for dates;

    (b) Check with client – also book preparation appointment with client;

    (c) Book Court Reporter;

    (d) Send confirming letters to other parties and client; and

    (e) Make sure conference room is booked if Discovery held here.

11. Forward standard Examination for Discovery letter to client confirming dates and preparation appointment.

12. Complete preparation of trial book and have reviewed by lawyer.

13. Trial book and file to lawyer at least one day in advance of Examination For Discovery to ensure preparation.

14. After Discovery, include Discovery Exhibits, counsel notes, etc., in trial book – Make sure trial book up to date.

15. Forward copies of transcripts to client for review and comment with covering letter. Ask client to complete responses to undertakings as soon as possible.

16. Diarize for follow-up.

17. Place original transcripts in separate folio. Punched copies to be put in trial book.

18. Write to opposing counsel requesting responses to undertakings in 30 days (or longer if lawyer requires).

19. Phone opposing counsel re responses to undertakings. If not available, prepare application to compel response.

20. When undertakings arrive:

    (a) Lawyer to review;

    (b) Response to be placed in trial book;

    (c) Copy to file; and

    (d) Copy of Undertakings to be forwarded to client for review and comment.

21. Prepare and sign Certificate of Readiness and forward to opposing counsel – Follow-up with opposing counsel to ensure that it is signed in a timely fashion.

22. File Certificate of Readiness and Record to set trial date.

23. Schedule pre-trial if required.

24. Send standard letter to client regarding trial date and procedure.

25. Lawyer to review file for trial preparation.

26. Set appointments for trial preparation for client and witnesses.

APPENDIX 3F

Litigation Checklist – Employer

1.   **ARE WE FREE TO ACT?**

_____ Do we act for the proposed opposite parties?

Is there any possibility that any of our regular clients will be brought into the action by way of third party proceedings or otherwise?

2.   **CLIENT**

_____ Advised of fee basis?

_____ Advised of economics of wrongful dismissal litigation?

_____ Extent of your authority defined?

_____ Advised of possible length of litigation?

_____ Advised that you cannot guarantee success?

_____ Terms of retainer confirmed in writing?

If corporate client, consider obtaining directors resolution confirming:
_____ Conditions of retainer
_____ From whom instruction may be taken
_____ To whom reports may be made

_____ Has likelihood of successful collection of judgment been canvassed with client?

NOTE: Client should be kept informed of each step as matter progresses. All instructions should be confirmed in writing.

3.   **LIMITATION DATES**

_____ Enter in Limitations Diary

_____ Enter in own diary

_____ Note date on face of file

_____ As each date is met, enter new limitation date

_____ Treat Rule 11 as limitation date for service of Statement of Claim

4. **ARE THERE CONDITIONS PRECEDENT TO ACTION?**

_____ Time limits on giving notice if Defendant is suing municipal or government bodies;

_____ Contractual conditions precedent such as demand or proof of loss or exhausting remedies;

_____ Consent to sue needed?

5. **JURISDICTION**

_____ Is action properly brought in Alberta? Can all defendants be served here?

_____ Any chance Federal Court involved?

_____ Exclusive jurisdiction in other body like Workers' Compensation Board or Public Utilities Board?

6. **CAPACITY**

_____ (e.g., infant, mental incompetent, estate, partnership?)

7. **INDEMNITY**

_____ Does client have any right of indemnity, contribution or right to third party or other party? Or insurance?

8. **CRIMINAL OR OTHER PROCEEDINGS OR HEARINGS**

_____ Have there been any?

9. **WORKERS' COMPENSATION ACT**

_____ Are any claimants covered?

_____ Has consent been obtained?

10. **AUTHORITY TO ACT**

_____ (e.g., Director's resolution for corporate client)

11. **COMPULSORY JOINDER**

_____ Are there any Joint parties?

12. **HAVE PARTIES BEEN PROPERLY IDENTIFIED?**

_____ Proper corporate name?

_____ Limited liability – any arguments against?

_____ Partnership (join all parties)?

_____ Agency?

_____ Guarantees?

_____ Representative of estate deceased?

13. **REVIEW ALL RELEVANT STATUTES AND REGULATIONS**

List below all prevalent statutes and regulations:

_____ All limitation periods noted and diarized

4

SPECIAL PRACTICE ISSUES

4.1 LIMITATION PERIODS

o Typical limitation periods for wrongful dismissal and related claims include:

  o Wrongful dismissal action/breach of contract – 6 years from date of termination of employment: *Limitation of Actions Act* ("*L.A.A.*"), R.S.A. 1980, c. L-15, s. 4(1)(c).

  o Tort action, such as negligent misrepresentation – 2 years from discovery of cause of action: *L.A.A.*, s. 51.

  o Human rights complaint – one year from actions giving rise to complaint: *Human Rights, Citizenship and Multiculturalism Act*, R.S.A. 1980, c. H-11.7, s. 19(2).

  o Minimum legislated standards under the *Employment Standards Code* ("*E.S.C.*"), S.A. 1988, c. E-10.2, such as statutory notice of termination, wages, overtime, vacation pay, general holiday pay and other entitlements – 1 year, with the possibility of one additional year in the discretion of the director (s. 98).

4.2 UNIONS

o When the employee is represented by a union and covered under a collective agreement, the courts do not have jurisdiction to entertain a common law action: *Weber v. Ontario Hydro* (1995), [1995] 2 S.C.R. 929; *St. Anne Nackawic Pulp & Paper Co. v. C.P.U., Loc. 219* (1986), [1986] 1 S.C.R. 704; *Oliva v. Strathcona Steel Manufacturing Inc.* (1986), Alta. L.R. (2d) 193 (C.A.), leave to appeal to S.C.C. refused (1987), 50 Alta. L.R. (2d) xlvii (S.C.C.).

o A grievance for wrongful dismissal must be filed by the union under the collective agreement. Given the tight time lines typically provided for under the grievance and arbitration procedure, the grievance should be filed as soon as possible after termination of employment.

o Where the union does not support the grievance, it may give rise to an unfair representation complaint before the Alberta Labour Relations Board. See: Alberta *Labour Relations Code*, S.A. 1988, c. L-1.2, s. 151.

o When the complaint is successful, the Board has the authority to extend time limits under the collective agreement for filing of the grievance.

4.3 INTERNATIONAL EMPLOYMENT AND CONFLICT OF LAWS

o Difficult issues arise in international employment situations, such as:

o Who is the real employer? It may be that the Canadian parent, or related company, and the offshore company are both employers. See: Section 2.6.1, *supra*, and *Bagby v. Gustavson International Drilling Co.* (1980), 24 A.R. 181 (C.A.); *Campbell v. Pringle & Booth Ltd.* (1988), 30 C.C.E.L. 156 (Ont. H.C.).

o Which law applies? Canadian law or law of foreign jurisdiction? Arguably, where the employee is hired in Alberta by an Alberta-based company, the courts will imply that the intention of the parties was to be governed by Alberta law. See: *Campbell v. Pringle & Booth Ltd.* (1988), 30 C.C.E.L. 156 (Ont. H.C.).

o Does Alberta or federal legislation apply to the employment in the foreign jurisdiction? That is, do federal or provincial employment standards and human rights apply? See: Levitt, *The Law of Dismissal in Canada* (2d ed.) (Canada Law Book, 1992), §110; *Hill v. W.P. London & Associates Ltd.* (1986), 13 C.C.E.L. 194 (Ont. H.C.).

4.4 MULTIPLE PARTIES

o The plaintiff may bring the action against one or more corporate defendants, and join one or more individuals in the cause of action for wrongful dismissal. See: *Olson v. Sprung Instant Greenhouses Ltd.* (1985), 41 Alta. L.R. (2d) 325 (Q.B.).

4.4.1 RELATED COMPANIES

o Where the employee is involved in one or more related companies, then all may be joined in the wrongful dismissal action as employers.

o Even where the employee has not worked for a parent corporation, where the parent is clearly in control it may be an employer pursuant to the common law.

4.4.2 JOINING INDIVIDUALS WITH THE EMPLOYER

o Where directors or officers act beyond their duties, they may be personally liable for inducing breach of contract or other tort actions. In such cases, the directors and officers may be personally named as defendants together with the company.

o Similarly, where employment appraisals or evaluations are carried out maliciously and in bad faith, this may give rise to an action in defamation where the individual responsible for the appraisal may be personally named.

4.5 SUCCESSORSHIP

o In a successorship situation the employee may name both the predecessor and the successor company.

o In most successorship situations, the new owner will have assumed the employee's contract, including the obligations as to dismissal, unless there are clear terms to the contrary. Absent a definite act or agreement to assign, an assignment or novation will be implied where the worker continues to provide services as before which are accepted by the new owner.

o Where there is uncertainty as to the successor company's obligations, the employee should join the predecessor company and the successor in the same action.

o Under Alberta's *E.S.C.*, the employee's service with a predecessor company is deemed to be continued with the successor company for the purposes of the minimum statutory entitlements. See: *E.S.C.*, s. 11.

o Where the court holds that there is no assignment or novation of the employment contract, a successor employer is not directly liable for the employee's damages for wrongful dismissal. This is particularly true where the selling employer terminated all employment contracts and paid severance pay. See: *White v. Stenson Holdings Ltd.* (1983), 1 C.C.E.L. 21 (B.C.S.C.).

4.6 INSOLVENT OR BANKRUPT EMPLOYER

o The appointment of a receiver/manager by court order or instrument may result in the termination of the contract of employment. The receiver/manager must be careful in continuing the employment of any of the employees, otherwise it may give rise to continued employment obligations of the successor. See: *Gresmak v. Yellowhead Town & Country Inn* (1989), 77 C.B.R. (N.S.) 245 (B.C. Co. Ct.).

o If the receiver/manager enters into contracts of employment with the former employees, then the receiver/manager becomes the employer.

o An assignment in bankruptcy operates as a dismissal from employment. See: *Bryant Isard & Co., Re* (1922), 3 C.B.R. 352 (Ont. H.C.); *Rizzo & Rizzo Shoes Ltd. (Receiver of) v. Rizzo & Rizzo Shoes Ltd. (Trustee of)* (1991), [1991] 6 W.W.R. 62 (Alta. Q.B.).

o In addition to the court action, in the case of a receivership or bankruptcy, the employee should file a claim with the receiver or trustee. Depending on the receivership order, leave of the court may be required.

5

DISCOVERY

o The purpose of the discovery process is to discover the other side's case, understand and evaluate the issues, seriously consider and explore settlement, and prepare for trial. Discovery includes, discovery of documents and examinations for discovery.

5.1 DISCOVERY OF DOCUMENTS

o This involves service of the demand for discovery and notice to produce, the preparation and filing of an affidavit of documents, and the production of all relevant documents.

o It is important to complete this process prior to examination for discovery for a number of reasons:

  o Review of all relevant documents enables legal counsel to prepare for the examination for discovery.

  o Review of the documents together with the client facilitates preparation of the client and legal counsel.

  o Each party to the action who has been served with a demand for discovery and notice to produce must prepare, file and serve an affidavit of documents which discloses all documents relating to any matter in issue in the action, including documents which are or have been in the party's possession, control or power. See: Alberta *Rules of Court*, RR. 186-199.

5.1.1   EMPLOYEE

o Send letter to client regarding production of documents. See: Appendix 5A – Letter to Plaintiff re Production of Documents.

o Once all relevant documents have been assembled, review all documents for relevance and privilege, and arrange in chronological order.

o Then prepare the affidavit listing the date, author and recipient, and type of document. This may be prepared by a clerk or law student and reviewed by the responsible lawyer.

o The draft affidavit of production should be forwarded to the client for review.

o The documents may be arranged in binders and tabbed. This can expedite the discovery process where counsel agree that the documents may be referred to by tab number and deemed to be marked for the purposes of examination for discovery.

o Once the affidavit of documents has been finalized with the client, it should be sworn, filed and served.

o Alternatively, with the agreement of the opposing counsel, a draft affidavit may be forwarded together with photocopies of all producible documents. Arrangements can then be made to have the affidavit sworn and filed on the day of the examination for discovery.

o Documents of the employee typical in a wrongful dismissal suit include:
  o the letter of termination;
  o any admissible severance offer;
  o job advertisement;
  o letters of hire;
  o employment contract;

- o employment policies;
- o cheque stubs;
- o termination pay stub;
- o evaluations;
- o letters of reference;
- o disciplinary letters;
- o written memos;
- o applicable portions of income tax returns;
- o job search portfolio; and
- o résumés

5.1.2 EMPLOYER

- o Send a letter to the employers' representative regarding production of documents. See: Appendix 5C – Letter to Employer re Discovery of Documents.

- o The employer's representative must be encouraged to produce all documents in the possession or power of the corporation. This may include production from former employees, agents, legal representatives, or third parties. It also includes not only the files of the individual dealing with legal counsel but also any other directors, officers or employees of the corporation.

- o Following delivery of the letter to the employer's representative, similar steps should be taken to prepare the affidavit of documents and produce relevant documentation.

- o Typical documents relevant to a wrongful dismissal litigation that may be in an employer's possession or power include:
  - o the employee's entire personnel file;
  - o job advertisements;
  - o letters of hire;
  - o the files of any company employee or third party involved in hiring;
  - o evaluations;
  - o disciplinary documents;

o notes and memoranda pertaining to interviews;
o letter of termination of employment;
o any admissible severance offers;
o employee benefits statements;
o policy manuals;
o personal diaries and notes kept by management, where these involve the former employee.

5.2   EXAMINATION FOR DISCOVERY

o The objectives of examination for discovery are:
  o As the name suggests, to enable the examining party to discover the other side's case.
  o To enable the examining party to obtain evidence from the party adverse in interest which can be read in as evidence at the trial.
  o To obtain admissions from the party adverse in interest which will advance the examining party's case and detract from the opponent's case.
  o To obtain sworn evidence that may be used to cross-examine that witness at trial.
  o To tie down the opponent to those facts which are obtained through examination for discovery.
  o To facilitate settlement.
  o To eliminate or narrow the issues for trial.

5.2.1   REPRESENTING THE EMPLOYEE

(a)   Preliminary Matters

(i)   Whom to examine

o A party may examine any party adverse in interest. Where it is a corporation, the party may examine any officer or employee. The cost of examining more than one employee is borne by the examining party without leave of the court. See: Alberta *Rules of Court*, R. 200(3).

o As the employer is usually a corporation, the plaintiff will
serve a notice to select. The corporate defendant will then
select its officer for the purposes of examination and will file
a notice of selection indicating the name.

o The officer's answers will be binding on the corporation.
The officer must have knowledge of the matters in question, and must obtain information from other employees of
the corporation and through the documents produced by
the corporation.

o If the defendant's selection of the officer is inappropriate,
given that the officer does not have knowledge of the matters in question, the plaintiff may apply to have an alternate
person appointed as the officer. See: R. 214(2); but see:
Leeds v. Alberta (Minister of the Environment) (1989), 68
Alta. L.R. (2d) 322 (C.A.).

o In addition to the officer, the plaintiff may also wish to examine an employee. In a wrongful dismissal action, this
could be a supervisor who has direct knowledge of the
facts leading to the termination of employment and other
matters.

o If an employee is to be examined as well as an officer, the
employee should be examined first.

o During the examination of the officer, the officer should be
asked to review the transcript from the examination for discovery of the employee and asked whether or not he or she
is prepared to adopt the transcript. If not, the officer should
be asked whether the information of the employee is the
information of the company. Using that approach, the
employee's answers will be binding on the company unless
specific information is not adopted.

o Then with respect to that information which is not adopted,
the examining party can canvass the reasons as to why it is
not. See: *Nova, an Alberta Corp. v. Guelph Engineering
Co.* (1986), 57 Alta. L.R. (2d) 15 (Q.B.); *Richards v.
Producers Pipelines Inc.* (1992), 44 C.C.E.L. 115 (Sask.
C.A.).

(ii)   Scheduling the examination for discovery

o Prior to scheduling the examination for discovery, the plaintiff must ensure that the following steps have been completed:

    o The pleadings have closed.

    o A demand for discovery and notice to produce has been served.

    o Affidavits of documents have been filed and served and producible documents have been inspected. Alternatively, by agreement of counsel, producible documents have been exchanged and there is an undertaking to provide a filed affidavit of documents during or following the examination for discovery.

    o A notice of selection selecting the defendant's officer has been filed, or alternatively counsel has been advised as to the name of the officer.

o The informal way of scheduling examinations for discovery is to arrange mutually convenient dates with the opposing counsel and arrange for them to produce their party voluntarily. The advantage of this approach is that it is scheduled at every one's convenience. The disadvantage is that if the other party does not appear, then the formal procedure must be followed before the court will enforce attendance.

o The formal procedure for initiating examination for discovery is to serve the other party with an appointment for examination together with the appropriate amount of conduct money.

o The conduct money represents the witness fees set out in Pt. 3 of Sched. E of the Alberta *Rules of Court*, together with allowable travelling expenses. If this cannot be accurately calculated, an amount should be agreed with the opposing counsel. Alternatively, the amount may be set by the taxing officer. See also: R. 204.

o Rule 216.1 provides the court with wide discretion in modifying conduct money and, where the defendant has corporate offices in Alberta and the officer or employee is required to travel from a distant location, the court may order a reduced amount of conduct money which does not fully cover the travelling expenses. See: *Royal Bank v. Parkway Country Plymouth-Chrysler Ltd.* (1982), 47 A.R. 218 (Master); but see: *F.G. Bradley Co. v. Maxwell Taylor's Restaurant Inc.* (1984), 53 A.R. 79 (Master).

o As a general rule, the plaintiff examines first followed by the defendant.

o Although examination for discovery may be conducted prior to ensuring a full discovery of documents, this is unwise because:
  o Counsel may not be properly prepared.
  o Your client may not be fully prepared.
  o Discovery of documents may make all or a portion of the examination for discovery unnecessary.

(b) Preparation

o In preparing the employer's officer and the employee for examination for discovery, legal counsel should do the following:
  o Review pleadings, memoranda of the information provided by client and witnesses, and all documents and relevant legal authority.
  o Prepare an outline to follow.

o In a wrongful dismissal action, discovery of the employer should include the following:
  o Confirming that the defendant is properly named and that the individual being examined is the defendant, or is produced as an officer or an employee of the corporate defendant.
  o Establishing that the defendant is the employer.
  o Establishing that the party being examined had direct knowledge or direct contact with the plaintiff.
  o Reviewing the steps taken by the party being examined to prepare for discovery, including to whom they spoke in the employer's organization and what documents were reviewed.

167

- o Recruitment and hiring.
- o Employment terms and conditions.
- o Position and duties of the plaintiff.
- o Reporting structure and compatibility with super-visors/colleagues.
- o Evaluations of the plaintiff.
- o Discipline of the plaintiff.
- o Circumstances leading to the dismissal of the plaintiff.
- o Salary and benefits of the plaintiff.
- o Notice of termination or pay in lieu of notice.
- o Reviewing the statement of defence and canvassing the evidence on which the opposite party is relying in support of its allegations.

(c)   Preparing your Client

- o Send a letter to your client outlining the examination for discovery process. See: Appendix 5B – Letter to Plaintiff re Examination for Discovery, and Appendix 5D – Letter to Employer re Examination for Discovery.

- o If you have access to a video tape on examination for discovery, invite the client to schedule an appointment to review it.

- o Schedule an appointment just prior to the commencement of the discovery to prepare the client and review the following:
  - o Highlight the examination for discovery process set out in the letter.
  - o Outline the factual and legal basis for the wrongful dismissal action and the nature of the defence. Review the statement of defence with your client.
  - o Review and obtain your client's comments on the producible documents (both plaintiff's and defendant's). This enables legal counsel to prepare for discovery of the other side and also prepares the client.
  - o Review critical areas by going through examination areas, including cross-examination.

o Answer any questions that the client might have.
o Provide your client with an outline of the examination for discovery questions that you will be asking the other side and ask for suggestions or comments.

(d) Organization of the Trial Brief

o Counsel should organize the trial brief from the outset of the case.

o There should be a clean copy of the brief and counsel's working copy. The additional volume and copies of documents is more than made up for with the efficiency of legal counsel and saving administrative headaches down the road.

o A full index of the trial brief should be prepared indicating the volume number and the title and the number of binders. This should be placed in the front of each binder followed by a particular index for that volume.

o The following should be included:
Volume 1 – Pleadings and court documents.
Volume 2 – Plaintiff's affidavit followed by tabbed producible documents.
        – Red Volume – Privileged documents.
Volume 3 – Defendant's affidavit followed by tabbed producible documents.
Volume 4 – A. Original examination for discovery transcripts.
        – B. Response to undertakings.
        – C. Discovery exhibits.
Volume 5 – Legal authority and memoranda.
Volume 6 – Witness briefs and counsel notes.
Volume 7 – Trial book:
        – A. Opening statement.
        – B. Examination-in-chief of plaintiff's witnesses, followed by notes from cross-examination.
        – C. Notes from examination-in-chief of defendant's witnesses, followed by cross-examination.

     – D. Closing argument
     – E. Legal authority

o Counsel should prepare a privileged working brief clearly marked and noted as "privileged".

o The working brief should consist of highlighted and annotated versions of the trial brief for counsel's purposes and can include the following:

    o Highlighted or annotated versions of the pleadings.
    o Interview notes as amended and updated.
    o Chronological and other lists relating to the issue.
    o Discovery outlines.
    o Counsel notes.
    o Both affidavits on production followed by either the full production or key annotated documents.
    o Witness statements.
    o A perpetual or topical calendar.

o Using properly bound, indexed and tabbed volumes of all of the producible documents, the documents can be referred to by their tab numbers in the plaintiff's or defendant's production and deemed to be marked for the purposes of examination for discovery. This saves a lot of time.

o In most cases, it is of great assistance to the client to prepare a brief consisting of the pleadings and tabbed volumes of the producible documents to assist in preparation and to follow during the examination for discovery.

(e)   Examination of the Defendant

(i)   Guidelines

o The following general guidelines should be followed for examination for discovery:

    o After the witness has been sworn, have the witness state his or her full name for the record and ask the witness on the record if he or she has been sworn.

o Open the discovery with a brief reference to the action number, judicial district and the style of cause.

o Confirm that the party being examined is the defendant, or, in the case of a corporate defendant, whether he or she is produced as an officer, employee or in some other capacity.

o Conduct a preliminary examination of the witness's background, position, personal characteristics, familiarity with the plaintiff and the facts of the case, and the preparation undertaken for examination for discovery.

o Conduct an examination on the documents and determine whether the production is complete.

o Do not attempt to keep *verbatim* notes during the discovery. Simply jot down important references for follow-up, be a good listener, and be flexible enough to examine important areas.

o Use the discovery to observe and assess the witness.

o Ask for undertakings where appropriate, but fully examine the witness as to his or her knowledge prior to allowing an undertaking.

o Use an organizational check-list to keep track of your progress and to ensure that all areas are covered.

o As the examining counsel, control the discovery.

o Direct and determine when discussion is on and off the record,

o As examining counsel, take the evidence from the witness. Discourage the opposite party's counsel from intervening or answering.

o However, where an answer from the opposing counsel is necessary, follow it up by asking if the witness adopts counsel's answer.

o Where the opposing counsel insists on intervening or answering, ask whether counsel would like to trade places with his or her client and be examined for discovery. If so, arrangement should be made for independent legal representation. If not, perhaps counsel could let the client answer the question unless there is a valid objection placed on the record.

o Where that does not work, consider adjourning the discovery pending an application to obtain the guidance of the court in the matter.

o As the examining counsel, there may be appropriate circumstances where the witness should be removed before the opposing counsel stipulates an objection. Otherwise the objection could become a prompter for the witness.

o Allow the opposing counsel to state any valid objections and briefly provide reasons for the objection. Recognize that the questions must be fair, relevant and capable of response.

o Do not argue the point with the opposing counsel, and if agreement cannot be reached regarding the validity of the objection, go on to another area of questioning and bring an application at a later date to compel response. Consider rephrasing the area of questioning so that it is not objectionable.

(ii)   Preliminary examination

o After the party to be examined is sworn, consider going through the following preliminary matters:

   o Get agreement of the other counsel to allow reference to documents by tab number in the plaintiff's/defendant's production, and by so referring to the documents they will be deemed to be marked for purposes of examination for discovery.

   o In appropriate cases, obtain agreement of the other counsel that all documents identified in a party's affidavit on production, all documents marked for purposes of examination for discovery, and all documents produced in response to undertakings shall be deemed to be admissible at trial without further proof, but either party may call further evidence to explain, expand upon, qualify or contradict the documents so admitted. This admission shall apply unless there is specific objection in writing by the opposite party through his or her counsel prior to trial.

o After the party to be examined has been sworn, go through preliminary matters followed by the substance of examination. See: Appendix 5E – Discovery Pattern – Defendant.

(A) EXAMINATION OF EMPLOYER OR OFFICER

o The courts in Alberta allow a full and complete discovery, but not a "fishing expedition". Relevant questions are those that may relate to any matter in issue and may advance or detract from either party's case. The pleadings generally frame the relevant issues.

o The defendant's officer must answer for the company. That may require reasonable enquiries of other employees, agents and third parties, where the officer has the power to so enquire. This may also involve searching for, reviewing and producing documents.

o The following areas of questioning are improper:
  o Unclear, double-barrelled or unfair questions.
  o Questions of law or opinion which are beyond the scope of the witness' expertise.
  o Hypothetical or speculative questions.
  o Irrelevant questions.
  o Questions about inadmissible evidence, such as privilege or without prejudice communication

o If a document is referred to which has not been produced and referred to by its tab number, it must be marked as a discovery exhibit or an exhibit for an identification.

○ However, even though the document has been referred to or identified in the discovery, it does not mean that it is admissible at trial without establishing the foundation for admissibility.

(B)   EXAMINATION OF OTHER EMPLOYEES

○ The plaintiff may also wish to examine an employee in addition to an officer. In a wrongful dismissal action this could be a supervisor who has direct knowledge of the facts leading to the termination of employment and other matters.

○ If an employee is to be examined as well as an officer, the employee should be examined first.

○ Consider examining an employee in addition to an officer where:
  ○ the officer does not have extensive knowledge in the matters and issues;
  ○ cause is an issue, so key employees and supervisors should be examined;
  ○ that employee's evidence may be critical.

5.2.2   REPRESENTING THE EMPLOYER

○ See "Preliminary Matters" in Section 5.2.1(a); Appendix 5C – Letter to Employer re Discovery of Documents; Appendix 5D – Letter to Employer re Examination for Discovery; and Appendix 5F – Discovery Pattern – Plaintiff.

5.3   TRANSCRIPT

○ Upon conclusion of the examination for discovery, the court reporter will ask each counsel whether he or she wishes to order a transcript. Where there is a reasonable chance that settlement could be achieved, postpone ordering a transcript until settlement negotiations have been exhausted. This could save your client the considerable disbursement expense of the discovery transcript.

o Once received, review the discovery transcript for any errors. If there are any errors, point these out in a letter to the court reporter, a copy of which is sent to the opposing counsel.

o Forward the transcripts from the examination for discovery to your client for review. Have the client advise you immediately as to any errors in the transcript.

o Ask the client to make careful notes in his or her review of the transcript regarding any matters. These notes should be reviewed in preparation for trial.

o Store the original transcript so that it is readily available for trial.

o Insert copies of the transcripts in the trial brief.

APPENDIX 5A

Letter to Plaintiff re Production of Documents

Lawyer's Name
Direct Line: *
Our File No.: *

*

*

Dear *:

Re: *

We have reached the stage in your action where we are obligated to prepare, swear, file and serve an Affidavit of Documents.

An Affidavit of Documents sets out those documents that are now or have been in your possession, or are within your power or control, and that may shed light on the case at trial. This includes documents that you once had, but were aware of and may be located somewhere else or may have since been destroyed. It also may include documents which are in someone else's hands, but which you are able to obtain by requesting them. In addition to printed documents, it could include photographs, pictures, charts, graphs, voice tapes, video tapes and even computer data. Even handwritten notes and memoranda would qualify whether they are clear or not.

You must swear that aside from the documents listed in the Affidavit, there are no other documents whatsoever relating to the matters in question in the action. If for some reason we neglect to include a particular document, and this matter proceeds to trial without us disclosing that document to the other side and filing a Supplementary Affidavit of Documents, we may be prevented from relying on that document at trial, or we may be penalized in some way by the Court. It is therefore critical that the Affidavit be complete to the best of your knowledge, information and belief.

You are required under our Court rules to conduct a diligent search of your records (and your company records) and to make appropriate inquiries of others who may have information as to relevant documents, in order to swear your Affidavit. You must also turn your mind as to whether or not there are documents which were once in your possession, control, or power which have since been either lost or are with some other party.

176

We must produce all relevant documents, regardless of whether you think they hurt your case or are confidential. The decision as to what constitutes an irrelevant or legally privileged document is left to your lawyer and ultimately the Court.

We enclose a draft Affidavit of Documents which lists all of the relevant documents which we currently have in our possession. In addition to those documents listed in the draft Affidavit, in our view the following would be relevant and producible if they are in your possession or power:

1. Letters of application for employment.

2. Any letters of other documents pertaining to your job search.

3. Any records or other correspondence between you and * regarding your job, your performance on the job, and so forth.

4. If you have since obtained alternative employment since the termination of your employment from *, any letters or other documents from your new employer outlining the job and your remuneration and other benefits.

If you have any documents which would fit in with the above description, I would appreciate it if you could send me these documents, as well as any other documents in your possession that bears on this matter as soon as possible. I will then review all of the additional documents and revise the Affidavit of Documents for your signature.

If there are no additional documents, please review the Affidavit of Documents as soon as possible and advise me as to whether it is complete. If I do not hear from you on or before *, I will assume that it is complete and remit it to the other side. I will make arrangements with the opposing counsel for you to execute the Affidavit of Documents at your Examination for Discovery. If this is not acceptable to the opposing counsel, my secretary, *, will make arrangements with you to attend at our offices in order to execute the Affidavit of Documents. We will then proceed to have the Affidavit of Documents filed and served on the opposing counsel.

We have also been provided with a Notice from the other side which requires us to select the representative from * who will act as the "officer" at the Examination for Discovery. This should be someone who is familiar with the issues, but who will also be able to answer on behalf of the company. The answers of the officer at the Examination for Discovery are binding on the company. We will of course be working with the officer to ensure that he or she is adequately prepared for the Examination. We recommend that the officer be either * or you. Please advise us as soon as possible.

We look forward to your response. In the meantime, should you have any questions or concerns, please do not hesitate to contact us. We advise Examinations for Discovery have been scheduled at our offices on * commencing at * for a full day. As an officer for * will be attending from *, they are entitled to conduct money in the amount of $* which you are responsible for. If you are successful at trial, you will be reimbursed in the form of party/party costs at the discretion of the Court. Please confirm your availability with my secretary, *, at *.

Yours truly,

LAW FIRM NAME

Lawyer's Name

Enclosure

APPENDIX 5B

Letter to Plaintiff re Examination for Discovery

Lawyer's Name
Direct Line: *
Our File No.: *

[Date]

[Employee's Name and Address]

*

*

*

Dear *:

Re: *

We confirm that we have arranged an appointment for your Examination for Discovery on * commencing at 10:00 a.m. in our offices.

I should appreciate meeting with you at 8:30 a.m. on *, and at that time I will answer any questions that you might have and will prepare you for the upcoming examination.

The Examination for Discovery provides each party with the opportunity to ask questions of the opposing party concerning the claim or the defence in the law suit. The main purpose, as the name suggests, is to "discover" the other side's case. Later, at trial, the Examination for Discovery can be used against the opposite party for the following:

1. To read in evidence from the Examination for Discovery transcript (usually admissions made by the other side); and,

2. To cross-examine the witness who appeared at the discovery if his or her evidence at trial is different from the evidence at the Discovery.

A party cannot use their own Examination for Discovery transcript in further proceedings, and can only use the transcript of the opposite party.

Furthermore, there is no obligation to file the transcript at the court house or to use it in further proceedings. For example, the opposite party may, as a general rule, select those parts of the transcript that help their case, and ignore those parts which hurt it. This is important to remember. When you are being examined - it is the other side's discovery. Your obligation is to listen to the other side's questions, and, if I do not object to the question, to answer it honestly and directly.

The Examination for Discovery is held before a Court Reporter who is authorized by the court to take evidence under oath. The examination will take place in a conference room at this office. The only people present will be you, the opposing counsel, a representative of the Defendant, and myself. The Court Reporter will administer an oath to the parties being examined. Firstly, I will be given an opportunity to examine the other party's officer. The Court Reporter will record my questions and his/her answers verbatim. The reporter records everything said, unless the parties agree to go off the record.

You are entitled to be present during the examination of the other parties. You are not entitled to make any remarks during my examination of the opposing party. However, I would like you to take notes and advise me during various breaks as to your version of certain facts, and I will ask you to point out areas that you feel should be examined. As a general rule, just before I finish my examination of the opposing party, I will take a brief adjournment and ask you if there are any matters that I may have missed or should explore further.

Following the examination of the opposing party, the opposing party's counsel will have an opportunity to examine you. You will be required to respond to the opposing counsel's questions in a direct and truthful manner. Again, the Court Reporter will record the other lawyer's questions and your answers word for word.

At times during the examinations, I may instruct you not to answer particular questions. My reasons for doing so are twofold. Firstly, certain questions are off-limits as a matter of law, and it is improper for the opposing counsel to ask them. Secondly, I may have tactical reasons for instructing you to remain silent, even if you know the answer. You must not answer a question that I have instructed you not to answer. A good practice is to pause for a moment after a question has been asked. This gives me an opportunity to determine whether I should object to the question, and it also gives you an opportunity to get the answer clear in your mind before you respond.

If either party refuses or neglects to answer certain questions, the other party's lawyer may bring a motion compelling re-attendance to answer all or some of these questions. Although we will address that issue when it arises, you should understand that you may be examined more than once.

It is a common practice where a party does not know the answer at the Examination for Discovery, to give an undertaking to check certain information and respond at a later date. This is known as "undertakings". If the party gives an undertaking, they will be given a reasonable period of time in which to respond in writing to the undertaking, and to provide the answer requested. Once the undertakings have been responded to, the party may be called by the opposing counsel for re-examination on the undertakings, and the Examination for Discovery would be scheduled again for that purpose. If a party has not responded to the undertakings within a reasonable period of time, the opposite party may bring an application to compel their response. It is best to prepare yourself for discovery well ahead of time, and to keep undertakings to a minimum. Generally, undertakings tend to slow litigation down.

Following the Examination for Discovery, the Court Reporter will prepare a transcript of the questions and answers. As a party to the action, you will be responsible for the Court Reporter's fees for the time spent at the Examination for Discovery and preparing the transcript. The average cost should be about $500 to $750 for each day of examination. At this time we anticipate that the Examination for Discovery in this action will take about one day. You will be asked to reimburse us for the Court Reporter's expense after we receive the transcript.

I am enclosing a Discovery instruction sheet of "Do's and Don'ts". Please review the instructions and contact me if you have any questions.

If you feel that you would like further information on the Examination for Discovery process, the firm has a video tape showing an examination, which illustrates a number of points to keep in mind. It takes about 1/2 hour to view it. If you feel that it would be helpful to see this, please schedule an appointment with my secretary and she will make the necessary arrangements.

I look forward to meeting with you again at our appointment prior to the Examination for Discovery at 8:30 on *.

Yours very truly,

LAW FIRM NAME

Lawyer's Name

enclosure

EXAMINATION FOR DISCOVERY

DO'S and DONT'S

1. **DO** remember the purpose of the Examination for Discovery. This could be summarized as follows:

(a) to **DISCOVER** the other side's case;

(b) to gain admissions from the other side which help you in your litigation;

(c) to tie the other side down to certain answers, and if they change their story at trial for cross-examination of that Party as a witness.

2. **DO** remember when you are examined that your Examination for Discovery transcript can only be used **against** you, and rarely in your favour. **DO** remember that it is the other side's Discovery when they are asking a question.

3. Understand the questions. If you do not understand, say so. Think before answering. **DO NOT** overstate your case. In very few cases you have to use the words "never" or "always".}

4. Be approximate concerning figures and distances.

5. *Never* guess.

6. **DON'T** be afraid to admit that you do not know or cannot remember. If you could find the answer out, it may be appropriate to give an undertaking, and if you cannot, say so.

7. Make your answers brief and direct. **DON'T VOLUNTEER ANYTHING** because it may allow the other counsel a chance to explore something which he had not thought of.

8. Tell the truth.

9. If I tell you **NOT** TO ANSWER, **DO NOT ANSWER.**

APPENDIX 5C

Letter to Employer re Discovery of Documents

Lawyer's Name
Direct Line: *
Our File No.: *

[Date]

PRIVATE & CONFIDENTIAL

[Employer's Name and Address]

Dear *:

Re: *

We enclose a copy of correspondence and document served on our office by [Name of Employee]'s counsel. Opposing counsel has also contacted our office in order to request all our documentation pertaining to this case.

We are now obligated to prepare, file and serve an Affidavit of Documents. An Affidavit of Documents sets out those documents that are now or have been in your possession, or are within your power or control, and that may shed light on the case at trial. This includes documents that you once had, but were aware of and may be located somewhere else or may have since been destroyed. It also may include documents which are in someone else's hands, but which you are able to obtain by requesting them. In addition to printed documents, it could include photographs, pictures, charts, graphs, voice tapes, video tapes and even computer data. Even handwritten notes and memoranda would qualify whether they are clear or not.

You must swear that aside from the documents listed in the Affidavit, there are no other documents whatsoever relating to the matters in question in the action. If for some reason we neglect to include a particular document, and this matter proceeds to trial without us disclosing that document to the other side and filing a Supplementary Affidavit of Documents, we may be prevented from relying on that document at trial, or we may be penalized in some way by the Court. It is therefore critical that the Affidavit be complete to the best of your knowledge, information and belief.

You are required under our Court rules to conduct a diligent search of your records (and your company records) and to make appropriate inquiries of others who may have information as to relevant documents, in order to swear your Affidavit. You must also turn your mind as to whether or not there are documents which were once in your possession, control, or power which have since been either lost or are with some other party.

183

We must produce all relevant documents, regardless of whether you think they hurt your case or are confidential. The decision as to what constitutes an irrelevant or legally privileged document is left to your lawyer and ultimately the Court.

We enclose a draft Affidavit of Documents which lists all of the relevant documents which we currently have in our possession. In addition to those documents listed in the draft Affidavit, in our view the following would be relevant and producible if they are in your possession or power:

- Application for employment and résumé
- Offer of employment
- Memoranda setting out reasons for termination
- Record of Employment
- Personnel file
- Diary and other personal notes related to the employee
- Letter of termination of employment

If you have any documents which would be relevant and producible in your possession or power, I would appreciate it if you could send me these documents as soon as possible. I will then review all of the additional documents and revise the Affidavit of Documents for your signature.

If there are no additional documents, please review the Affidavit of Documents as soon as possible and advise me as to whether it is complete. If I do not hear from you within two weeks, I will assume that it is complete and remit it to the other side. I will make arrangements with the opposing counsel for you to execute the Affidavit of Documents at your Examination for Discovery. If this is not acceptable to the opposing counsel, my secretary, *, will make arrangements with you to attend at our offices in order to execute the Affidavit of Documents. We will then proceed to have the Affidavit of Documents filed and served on the opposing counsel.

I look forward to hearing from you with respect to any further company documents or any questions you might have. Feel free to contact me at your earliest convenience.

Yours very truly,

LAW FIRM NAME

Lawyer's Name

Enclosure

APPENDIX 5D

Letter to Employer re Examination for Discovery

Lawyer's Name
Direct Line: *
Our File No.: *

[Date]

PRIVATE & CONFIDENTIAL

[Employer's Name and Address]

Dear *:

Re: *

We enclose a copy of correspondence and document served on our office by [Name of Employee]'s counsel. Opposing counsel has also contacted our office in order to arrange Examinations for Discovery in this matter. [He/She] has provided us with dates in * and * that would be convenient to both counsel, being *, * and *. Please advise as to your availability on these dates and if these dates are not convenient for you, please provide us with dates that you would be available for examination as the officer on behalf of [the Employer].

We are also required to select the representative from [Employer's Name] who will act as the "officer" at the Examination for Discovery. You are the best person to do this. The answers of the officer at the Examination for Discovery are binding on the company. We will of course be working with you to ensure that you are adequately prepared for the Examination.

We look forward to your response. In the meantime, should you have any questions or concerns, please do not hesitate to contact us. We advise Examinations for Discovery will be scheduled at opposing counsel's offices for a full day and I would appreciate meeting with the officer attending for Examinations at our offices at 8:30 a.m. that morning in order to prepare. Please confirm your availability with my secretary, *, at *.

The Examination for Discovery provides each party with the opportunity to ask questions of the opposing party concerning the claim or the defence in the law suit. The main purpose, as the name suggests, is to "discover" the other side's case. Later, at trial, the Examination for Discovery can be used against the opposite party for the following:

1. To read in evidence from the Examination for Discovery transcript (usually admissions made by the other side); and,

2. To cross-examine the witness who appeared at the discovery if his or her evidence at trial is different from the evidence at the Discovery.

A party cannot use their own Examination for Discovery transcript in further proceedings, and can only use the transcript of the opposite party.

Furthermore, there is no obligation to file the transcript at the court house or to use it in further proceedings. For example, the opposite party may, as a general rule, select those parts of the transcript that help their case, and ignore those parts which hurt it. This is important to remember. When you are being examined - it is the other side's discovery. Your obligation is to listen to the other side's questions, and if I do not object to the question, to answer it honestly and directly.

The Examination for Discovery is held before a Court Reporter who is authorized by the court to take evidence under oath. The examination will take place in a conference room at this office. The only people present will be you, the opposing counsel, a representative of the Defendant, and myself. The Court Reporter will administer an oath to the parties being examined. Firstly, I will be given an opportunity to examine the other party's officer. The Court Reporter will record my questions and his/her answers verbatim. The reporter records everything said, unless the parties agree to go off the record.

You are entitled to be present during the examination of the other parties. You are not entitled to make any remarks during my examination of the opposing party. However, I would like you to take notes and advise me during various breaks as to your version of certain facts, and I will ask you to point out areas that you feel should be examined. As a general rule, just before I finish my examination of the opposing party, I will take a brief adjournment and ask you if there are any matters that I may have missed or should explore further.

Following the examination of the opposing party, the opposing party's counsel will have an opportunity to examine you. You will be required to respond to the opposing counsel's questions in a direct and truthful manner. Again, the Court Reporter will record the other lawyer's questions and your answers word for word.

At times during the examinations, I may instruct you not to answer particular questions. My reasons for doing so are twofold. Firstly, certain questions are off-limits as a matter of law, and it is improper for the opposing counsel to ask them. Secondly, I may have tactical reasons for instructing you to remain silent, even if you know the answer. You must not answer a question that I have instructed you not to answer. A good practice is to pause for a moment after a question has been asked. This gives me an opportunity to determine whether I should object to the question, and it also gives you an opportunity to get the answer clear in your mind before you respond.

If either party refuses or neglects to answer certain questions, the other party's lawyer may bring a motion compelling re-attendance to answer all or some of these questions. Although we will address that issue when it arises, you should understand that you may be examined more than once.

It is a common practice where a party does not know the answer at the Examination for Discovery, to give an undertaking to check certain information and respond at a later date. This is known as "undertakings". If the party gives an undertaking, they will be given a reasonable period of time in which to respond in writing to the undertaking, and to provide the answer requested. Once the undertakings have been responded to, the party may be called by the opposing counsel for re-examination on the undertakings, and the Examination for Discovery would be scheduled again for that purpose. If a party has not responded to the undertakings within a reasonable period of time, the opposite party may bring an application to compel their response. It is best to prepare yourself for discovery well ahead of time, and to keep undertakings to a minimum. Generally, undertakings tend to slow litigation down.

Following the Examination for Discovery, the Court Reporter will prepare a transcript of the questions and answers. As a party to the action, you will be responsible for the Court Reporter's fees for the time spent at the Examination for Discovery and preparing the transcript. The average cost should be about $500 to $750 for each day of examination. At this time we anticipate that the Examination for Discovery in this action will take about one day. You will be asked to reimburse us for the Court Reporter's expense after we receive the transcript.

I am enclosing a Discovery instruction sheet of "Do's and Don'ts". Please review the instructions and contact me if you have any questions.

I look forward to hearing from you with respect to any further company documents, dates for Examinations for Discovery and confirmation of who the officer on behalf of [Employer's Name] will be.

Yours very truly,

LAW FIRM NAME

Lawyer's Name

Enclosure

APPENDIX 5E

Discovery Pattern – Defendant

1. **Preliminary Matters**

    o Identify action number, judicial district and style of cause.

    o Confirm that the Defendants are properly named.

    o Confirm that individual being examined is the Defendant, or if a corporate Defendant, whether produced as an officer, employee, or in some other capacity.

    o Confirm on the record that the witness took the oath.

    o Establish that the Defendant(s) was the employer of the Plaintiff and for which dates.

    o Ask the witness whether he or she knew the Plaintiff, for how long and in what context.

    o Ask the witness what they did in order to prepare for the Examination for Discovery. This should include details of all persons to whom they spoke, the general nature of the conversations, what documents were reviewed, and with whom they were reviewed.

2. **Background**

    o Review residence, education and training, employment history, résumé, present employment, title, position and duties.

    o Review the company's organizational chart at material times, supervisory relationship to the Plaintiff, whether personally involved in hiring, supervision, evaluation, discipline or discharge of Plaintiff, whether these general areas had to be discussed with others in the organization, and whether the witness had the final authority to documents.

    o Review the affidavit of documents and ask what files were reviewed in order to locate producible documents.

    o Ensure that personnel file was reviewed and that copies of salary and benefit information, awards, evaluations, warnings and discipline, and all other relevant documents have been produced.

    o Ensure that all diary notations (even in personal diaries), memoranda, handwritten notes, and any other records have been produced.

188

o If managerial staff or supervisors keep separate files, ensure that those have been reviewed and relevant documents produced.

o Ensure that relevant employee policy handbooks, benefit manuals, contracts, etc., have been produced.

o Where former employees or supervisors involved, ensure that they were contacted for any records and that those have been produced. If these records are not in their possession, determine where they are located and obtain an undertaking to review them and produce any relevant documentation.

o Ask for documents provided to the Canada Employment and Immigration Commission.

o Go through privileged documents and ensure claim of privilege is proper.

o Obtain details about documents where, although the document is privileged, the information inside may not be.

3. Hiring

o Determine:

o Was the Plaintiff recruited or enticed from secure employment?

o Did the Plaintiff respond to general advertising?

o Was the Plaintiff unemployed at the time of job interview?

o Did the Plaintiff work for a predecessor or related company?

o Review the job advertisement and hiring process.

o Review the offer of employment.

o What representations were made about the Plaintiff's job and the terms and conditions of employment?

o Was any written contract in place?

o Was the contract was given to the Plaintiff in advance of starting the job?

o Did the Plaintiff have the opportunity to discuss whether or not the contracts, terms and conditions were acceptable?

o Was the Plaintiff encouraged to obtain independent legal advice and had he or she the opportunity to do so?

o Who prepared the contract?

o Is it a standard form contract or must other employees sign it?

o Was a probationary period discussed and agreed to?

o Did training and orientation take place prior to commencement of the job?

o Identify all parties involved in the hiring process and ensure that their documents have been produced.

4. Employment Terms and Conditions

o Review all positions, titles, duties and reporting structure:

Date	Title	Duties	Reported to/ Title	Number of Employees Supervised	Promotion	Yes	No

o Obtain job descriptions if available.

o Confirm whether Plaintiff had any choice regarding promotions.

5. Final Positions and Duties

o Fully review final job title, job description, full details of all duties performed, supervisory responsibilities and reporting structure.

6. Compatibility with Others in the Work Place

o Ask whether the Plaintiff got along with supervisors and management. Get details regarding any concerns or problems.

190

o Ask whether Plaintiff got along with colleagues and explore details.

o Ask whether Plaintiff got along with customers, clients and so forth, and obtain all details.

7. Evaluations

o Fully review the evaluation process.

o Review all written evaluations.

o Ask whether follow-up interviews were done following the formal evaluation, and obtain all details.

o Review any merit increases and awards given.

8. Discipline

o Review any warnings or other discipline given to the employee.

o Fully canvass all details.

o Canvass the Plaintiff's response to discipline.

o Any discipline questioned or commented upon.

9. Compensation and Benefits

Review separately:

(a) Compensation

o Confirm salary.

o Overtime:

o Any accrued overtime that has not been paid?

o Average overtime on monthly/annual basis?

o Any time off in lieu of overtime agreement? If so, produce.

o Bonuses and other compensation:

o Details of bonus plan.

o Determine whether bonus is discretionary or non-discretionary.

(b) Benefits

o Group benefits:

o What group benefits does the employee receive?

o Convert or replace life insurance?

o Convert or replace long-term disability?

o Replace any other benefit? When?

o Pension:

o Details of claim for loss of pension.

o Any individual pension plan?

o Provide copies of pension plan and pension statements, other compensations/saving plans.

o Stock options? If so, produce stock option plan.

o Employee savings plan? If so, produce copy of plan.

o Any other plans? If so, produce copy.

o Automobile:

o Automobile benefit?

o Taxable benefit?

o Whether to reimburse employee for using automobile for work-related purposes or personal benefit?

o Obtain copies of benefits booklets.

o Obtain copies of benefit statements.

o Obtain copies of other plan documents.

o Obtain copies of relevant payroll records.

o Calculate total employer cost for employee's benefits on monthly/annual basis.

(c) Vacation

o Vacation entitlement?

o Any accrued vacation?

o Determine vacation policy.

10. Notice of Termination or Pay in Lieu of Notice

o Determine whether notice of termination of employment had been given:

    o Review written notice.

    o Explore exactly what was said if oral notice was given.

o If pay in lieu of notice, determine:

    o Amount.

    o Details of amount offered.

    o Confirm all details of amount employee received and for what reasons.

11. Other Issues

o Review statement of defence and examine on all issues raised in the statement of defence.

o Determine if there are any letters of reference provided to the employee at the employee's request or offered by the employer. If so, obtain copies.

o Any reference checks made? If so, what was said in response to the reference checks?

APPENDIX 5F

Discovery Pattern – Plaintiff

1. **Preliminary Matters**

   o Identify action number, judicial district and style of cause.

   o Confirm that individual being examined is the Plaintiff.

   o Confirm on the record that the witness took the oath.

   o Ask the plaintiff whether he or she spoke to any employees or former employees of the defendant company prior to or following commencement of the litigation regarding any matters involving their employment or termination of employment. If so, obtain details of all conversations.

2. **Background**

   o Review plaintiff's residence, education and training, employment history, résumé, present employment, title, position and duties.

   o Review affidavit of documents to confirm that all producible documents have been produced.

   o Ensure that all diary notations (even in personal diaries), memoranda, handwritten notes, and any other records have been produced.

   o Copies of salary and benefit information in employee's hands, including cheque stubs and benefit booklets.

   o Copies of any awards, evaluations, warnings and discipline in the Plaintiff's possession.

   o Copies of any job advertisements responded to.

   o Copy of a recent résumé used to obtain alternative employment.

   o Copies of any job applications and correspondence with potential employers.

   o Tax returns and related documentation for the period during employment with the defendant company and for the period of reasonable notice.

   o Any correspondence with unemployment insurance officials and related documentation.

o Correspondence with Employment Standards Branch.

o Documents related to any special damages claims, including job search expenses, benefit replacement, and pension loss.

o Documents related to any claim for general damages for mental suffering, punitive or aggravated damages.

o Go through privileged documents to ensure that privilege has been properly claimed.

o Obtain details about documents where, although the document is privileged, the information inside may not be.

3. Hiring

o Determine:

    o Whether the Plaintiff was recruited or enticed from secure employment.

    o Whether Plaintiff responded to general advertising.

    o Whether Plaintiff unemployed at time of job interview.

    o Whether Plaintiff worked for predecessor or related company.

    o Review job advertisement and hiring process.

    o Review offer of employment.

    o What representations were made about the Plaintiff's job and the terms and conditions of employment.

    o Whether any written contract in place.

    o Whether the contract was given to the Plaintiff in advance of starting the job.

    o Whether the Plaintiff had the opportunity to discuss if the contracts, terms and conditions were acceptable.

    o Whether the Plaintiff was encouraged to obtain independent legal advice and whether he or she the opportunity to do so.

    o Who prepared the contract.

    o Whether it is a standard form contract and whether other employees must sign it.

o Whether probationary period discussed and agreed to.

o Whether training and orientation took place prior to com-mencement of the job.

o Identify all parties involved in the hiring process.

o Review all documentataion provided by the company (or its agents) to the Plaintiff prior to acceptance of the offer of employment, includ-ing:

o Offer of employment.

o All correspondence between the company (and its agents) and the Plaintiff.

o Job description.

o Documentation related to salary and benefits.

o Any policies or contractual documents.

4. Employment Terms and Conditions

o Review all positions, titles, duties and reporting structure:

Date	Title	Duties	Reported to/ Title	Number of Employees Supervised	Promotion	Yes	No

o Review job descriptions and confirm with the Plaintiff as to whether:

> o he or she was given a copy.

> o it is an accurate job description.

> o the Plaintiff actually performed all of the duties set out in the job description.

o Confirm that the Plaintiff accepted all promotions and transfers. If the Plaintiff objected to any promotion or transfer, review all details.

5. Final Positions and Duties

o Fully review final job title, job description, full details of all duties performed, supervisory responsibilities and reporting structure.

6. Compatibility with Others in the Work Place

o Ask whether the Plaintiff got along with supervisors and management. Details regarding any concerns or problems.

o Ask whether Plaintiff got along with colleagues and explore details.

o Ask whether Plaintiff got along with customers, clients and so forth, and obtain all details.

7. Evaluations

o Fully review the evaluation process.

o Review all written evaluations.

o Ask whether follow-up interviews were done following the formal evaluation, and obtain all details.

o Review any merit increases and awards given.

o Review any diary notes, memoranda or other notations that the employee made during or subsequent to evaluations.

o Determine whether the Plaintiff ever made a formal or informal complaint following any evaluation and review any related documentation.

o Determine whether the Plaintiff felt that the evaluations were fair or not. If the Plaintiff did not feel that the evaluation was fair, what steps were taken to address his or her concerns.

8. Discipline

o Review any warnings or other discipline given to the Plaintiff.

o Fully canvass all details.

o Ask whether the Plaintiff felt the discipline was warranted or not.

o Ask whether the Plaintiff addressed any concerns regarding discipline with any supervisors, management or other employees of the company. If so, obtain details.

o If the Plaintiff did not question the discipline, why not?

o Any discipline questioned or commented upon.

9. Compensation and Benefits

Review separately:

(a) Compensation

o Confirm salary.

o Overtime:

o Any accrued overtime that has not been paid.

o Average overtime on monthly/annual basis:

o Any time off in lieu of overtime agreement? If so, produce.

o Bonuses and other compensation:

o Details of bonus plan.

o Determine whether discretionary or non-discretionary bonus.

(b) Benefits

o Group benefits:

o Group benefits that the employee receives?

o Convert or replace life insurance?

o Convert or replace long-term disability?

o Replace any other benefit? When?

198

o Pension:

> o Details of claim for loss of pension.
>
> o Any individual pension plan?
>
> o Provide copies of pension plan and pension statements, other compensations/saving plans.
>
> o Stock options? If so, produce stock option plan.
>
> o Employee savings plan? If so, produce copy of plan.
>
> o Any other plans? If so, produce copy.

o Automobile:

> o Automobile benefit?
>
> o Taxable benefit? (Review copies of tax return and T4 to determine amount related to personal benefit).
>
> o Whether to reimburse employee for using automobile for work-related purposes or personal benefit?

o Obtain copies of benefits booklets.

o Obtain copies of benefit statements.

o Obtain copies of other plan documents.

o Obtain copies of cheque stubs.

o Review employee and employer's share of benefit premiums.

(c) Vacation

> o Vacation entitlement?
>
> o Any accrued vacation?
>
> o Determine whether employee had permission to accrue vacation.
>
> o Determine whether employee was refused permission to take any vacation.
>
> o Determine whether it was the employee's choice to accrue vacation.

10. Review all Circumstances Leading to Termination of Employment

> o Review culminating incident and all details.
>
> o Review any related documentation.

o Review all meetings and discussions with management and supervisor regarding the culminating incident.

o If a meeting was held with the Plaintiff advising him or her of the termination of employment, obtail all details including when the meeting took place, where the meeting took place, who was present and exactly what was said.

o Review the employee's actions and activities following the meeting.

o If damages for mental discress claimed:

   o Determine whether the mental distress arose from the actions of the company management. If so, obtain all details.

   o Nature of mental distress.

   o Doctor, psychologist or other counselling received for mental distress.

   o Whether any medication prescribed.

   o Details of treatment and prognosis.

   o Effect of mental distress on the Plaintiff's personal life and family.

11. Notice of Termination or Pay in Lieu of Notice

o Determine whether notice of termination of employment had been given:

   o Review written notice.

   o Explore exactly what was said if oral notice was given.

   o If pay in lieu of notice, determine:

      o Amount.

      o Details of amount offered.

      o Confirm all details of amount Plaintiff received and for what reasons.

      o Determine whether the Plaintiff filed a claim with Employment Standards Branch because of failure to provide written notice of termination of employment and, if so, obtain all details and review all related documentation.

200

12. Search for Alternative Employment

o Review all job advertisements responded to.

o Review all contacts made to obtain alternative employment.

o Review any training or courses taken.

o Review any self-employment and details.

o Review any volunteer work that was undertaken and details. Ascertain why remuneration was not given.

o Review any work performed for family members, relatives or friends whether compensation received or not. Ascertain whether compensation is expected.

o Review all correspondence with potential employers.

o Review any relevant correspondence with unemployment insurance authorities.

o Review income tax returns for period of reasonable notice.

o If self-employed, review all relevant financial statements, accounting records, invoices and other relevant documents. Obtain tax returns related to self-employment.

o If new job obtained, confirm all details including date of commencement, position and duties. Obtain all details regarding remuneration and benefits and review any related documentation.

13. Other Issues

o Review the statement of claim and examine any other issues raised in the statement which have not been covered.

o Determine whether the employee requested any references or letters of reference. If so, obtain copies.

o Any reference checks made? If so, whether the Plaintiff was satisfied that the company was fair in its response to any reference checks. If no, obtain all details.

6

GETTING READY

6.1 UNDERTAKINGS

o If the party being examined at discovery must obtain certain
  documents or information from another individual, then it is
  appropriate to ask for an undertaking to obtain the information and advise the counsel conducting the examination.
  This may limit the requirement for further personal attendance at the examination for discovery and expedite the
  pre-trial process.

o The opposing counsel must first consider whether the undertaking is appropriate. If the information requested is appropriate, the undertaking should be given if it is one that
  the client can reasonably perform. If counsel is unsure, the
  undertaking may be taken under advisement.

o An undertaking taken under advisement should either be
  responded to or the reasons for not responding should be
  clearly articulated to the opposing counsel in writing. Where
  the undertaking requested is improper, it should be refused
  and the reasons for the refusal clearly stated on the record.

o Counsel requesting an undertaking should clearly state on
  the record the undertaking which has been requested.

o The agreement to provide the undertaking must be clearly
  granted by the opposing counsel for the party being examined.

o Counsel should record all undertakings given during the examination for discovery. Standard forms for that purpose are available from most court reporters.

o As soon as examinations for discovery have been completed, a standard letter should be sent to the opposing counsel outlining the undertakings which have been requested and requesting a response within 30 days of the letter.

o This should be followed up with a personal inquiry of the opposing counsel to determine the progress of the undertakings. If there is an unreasonable delay in responding to the undertakings, consideration should be given to a court application to compel response.

o The client should be encouraged to begin preparation to respond to the undertakings as soon as the examination for discovery has been concluded.

o The responses should be prepared in draft form and reviewed with counsel prior to finalizing the response in writing and forwarding it together with supporting documents to the opposing counsel.

o Once the examination for discovery transcripts arrive, they should be forwarded to the client. The client should be asked to review list of undertakings at the back of the examination for discovery and respond to them as soon as possible.

o Once the undertakings have been responded to, they should be reviewed. Consideration should be given as to whether further examination is necessary on the responses to the undertakings.

o The undertaking should be filed in the trial brief behind the applicable examination for discovery transcript.

6.1.1 EMPLOYEES

o Typical undertakings that an employee will usually have to provide include:

  o Evidence of job search and related records.
  o Income tax returns, particularly for the period after dismissal.
  o Receipts and other documents in support of damages claim.
  o Once alternative employment has been obtained, all documents related to the position, compensation and benefits.

6.1.2 EMPLOYER

o The undertakings of the employer are more extensive, particularly where the employer is a large organization and the area of the examination covers additional supervisors and management, a broad range of corporate documents, and perhaps the information that can only be obtained from offices outside the immediate area.

o Typical undertakings of an employer may include:

  o Production of additional documents arising from information requested at examination for discovery;
  o Obtaining information from other directors, officers, management, or employees of the corporate defendant;
  o Reviewing company records in order to ascertain or obtain further information;
  o Making inquiries of third parties to obtain relevant information and documents.

6.2 SUPPLEMENTARY AFFIDAVIT OF DOCUMENTS

o If further relevant documents come to the attention, possession or power of a party, these must be disclosed through a supplementary affidavit of documents which should be filed and served at the earliest possible opportunity.

o Failure to do this will mean that the party cannot introduce such documentation as evidence in trial without leave of the court.

o The supplementary affidavit of documents should begin where the other affidavit has left off.

o Counsel must ensure that any document produced in response to an undertaking should be listed in a supplementary affidavit.

6.3   SUMMARY JUDGMENT

o Where there are no serious issues of liability in dispute, counsel should consider bringing an application for summary judgment.

o The summary judgment process provides an expedited and straight-forward procedure to obtain a judgment and assessment by the court in a timely fashion.

o While it has been successful in other jurisdictions, the summary judgment process is rarely resorted to in Alberta. This may be because there are serious issues of trial or law in dispute, there is uncertainty regarding the period and the duty to mitigate, and the length of the pre-litigation process, compared to other provinces, is relatively short.

o In any event, given the difficult economic circumstances that the plaintiff faces, it may be worthwhile to recommend the summary judgment process where the only issue is the amount of reasonable notice and quantum of damages.

6.4   MINI-TRIAL

o The Alberta Court of Queen's Bench has introduced the mini-trial procedure to afford parties the opportunity to outline all of the key facts and legal principles in support of their positions.

o A judge will then consider all of the circumstances and provide his or her opinion on the case with supporting reasons. The parties may agree in advance to be bound by the decision of the mini-trial judge or at least fully consider the judge's conclusion in an effort to settle the outstanding claim.

o This procedure can be effective where all parties are prepared to co-operate and respect the judge's decision. It can save considerable time and expense and may facilitate the parties reaching agreement regarding the issues.

o The disadvantage of the mini-trial procedure is that it is not binding. Therefore, regardless of the judge's opinion during the course of the mini-trial, any of the parties may wish to proceed to trial.

APPENDIX 6A
Letter to Client following Examination for Discovery

Lawyer's Name
Direct Line: *
Our File No.: *

[Date]

[Address of Client]

Dear *:

Re: *

We enclose copies of the Examination for Discovery transcripts of the Examinations held [Date]. You will note at the end of the transcript of your examination there is a list of the Undertakings to be provided. Kindly provide your responses to these Undertakings as soon as possible in order that we might keep the matter proceeding expeditiously. Please give me a call should you have any questions or concerns in this regard.

Yours very truly,

LAW FIRM NAME

Lawyer's Name

enclosure

APPENDIX 6B
Response to Undertakings

Lawyer's Name
Direct Line: *
Our File No.: *

[Date]

[Address of Opposing Counsel]

Dear *:

Re: *

We are now in receipt of the transcripts from the Examinations for Discovery held on *. We would ask that you provide your client's responses to undertakings as soon as possible, in any event on or before *.

Yours very truly,

LAW FIRM NAME

Lawyer's Name

enclosure

APPENDIX 6C
Application for Summary Judgment

IN THE COURT OF QUEEN'S BENCH OF ALBERTA
JUDICIAL CENTRE OF *

B E T W E E N:

[Name]

Plaintiff

- and -

[Name]

Defendant

NOTICE OF MOTION

TAKE NOTICE in that an application will be made by the Plaintiff before the presiding Master in Chambers on [Date] at [Time] in the [Fore/After]noon, or so soon thereafter as counsel may be heard, at [Address of Court House], for summary judgment on the claim of the Plaintiff in the Statement of Claim.

AND FURTHER TAKE NOTICE that the Applicant relies on the following documentary evidence in support of his application:

1. The Affidavit of [Name], filed;

2. The Affidavit of [Name], filed; and

3. The pleadings filed herein.

FURTHER TAKE NOTICE that the grounds upon which the Plaintiff relies in support of this application are:

1. The Defendant has no defence to the claims in the Statement of Claim;

2. Rule 159 of the Alberta *Rules of Court*.

DATED at the [City/Town] of [Place], in the Province of Alberta, this [Date].

NAME OF LAW FIRM

Per: _____

Solicitors for the Plaintiff

IN THE COURT OF QUEEN'S BENCH OF ALBERTA
JUDICIAL CENTRE OF *

B E T W E E N:

[Name]

Plaintiff

- and -

[Name]

Defendant

AFFIDAVIT

I, [Name] of the [City/Town] of [Place] in the Province of Alberta, [Occupation], MAKE OATH AND SAY:

1. I am [Position] [With/Of] the Plaintiff herein and as such have personal knowledge of the matters hereinafter deposed to.

2. I was employed with the Defendant [Name] from [Date] to [Date] as a [Position].

3. As a [Position], I was responsible for [Particular Job Duties], and I am familiar with the system and method adopted by the Defendant in [Specific Tasks, e.g., the ordering and supplying of goods and merchandise, the invoicing and pricing of goods, etc.].

4. Prior to being a [Position], I worked as a [Position2] with the Defendant. My general duties in this position included [Particular Job Duties].

5. Over the past [Number] years with the Defendant, I have received a number of commendations and positive feedback from my employer, including [Specific Feedback, e.g., positive reviews, employee of the month awards, etc.]. Attached herewith as Exhibit "A" to this my Affidavit is a true copy of said commendations.

6. On [Date], I found out I was pregnant. Being wary of how this may affect my employment, I decided to wait until [Date] to inform the Defendant. Attached herewith as Exhibit "B" to this my Affidavit is a true copy of letter I wrote to the company explaining my situation.

7. On [Date], [Name of Officer of Defendant], who is a [Officer's Position] with the Defendant, came into my office and informed me that my services were no longer required with the firm and my employment was terminated

effective immediately. When I asked what was the reason for my dismissal, [Mr./Ms.][Last Name of Officer] said it was due to my incompetence on the job. [He/She] informed me that I would receive my vacation pay and benefits payable to the end of the day.

8. On [Date], [Name of Officer of Defendant] provided me with an Agreement to sign, releasing the Defendant from any liability for my dismissal. In return, [Name of Officer] told me the company would pay me my annual bonus. I refused to sign the Agreement, which angered [Name of Officer]. Attached herewith as Exhibit "C"to this my Affidavit is a true copy of the said Release Agreement.

9. I cleaned out my office on [Date] and have had no further contact with anyone at [Name of Defendant].

10. Due to the stress from losing my job, my doctor, [Name of Doctor], has informed me that my blood pressure was at a "serious level" and the foetus I was carrying was undergoing significant trauma. He ordered me to remain home in bed for the next month, during which time I could not look for alternative employment. As a result of the financial pressures my family experienced, I underwent severe mental stress and emotional pain. Attached herewith as Exhibit "D" to this my Affidavit is a true copy of my doctor's assessment report.

11. I have never received a negative performance evaluation or adverse feedback from [Name of Defendant] during my [number] years of employment. No one at the company has even mentioned the word "incompetence" to me until the day of my dismissal.

12. I make this Affidavit in support of an application for summary judgment pursuant to Rule 159(1).

SWORN BEFORE ME at the [City/Town] of   )
[Place], in the Province of Alberta this [Date].   )
)
)
_____   )
A COMMISSIONER FOR OATHS in and for   )   _____
the Province of Alberta whose commission   [Name]
expires on [Date].

IN THE COURT OF QUEEN'S BENCH OF ALBERTA
JUDICIAL CENTRE OF *

B E T W E E N:

[Name]

Plaintiff

- and -

[Name]

Defendant

JUDGMENT

UPON the application of the Plaintiff for summary judgment pursuant to Rule 159(1); AND UPON reading the Affidavit of [Name]; AND UPON hearing the submissions of counsel for the Plaintiff and for the Defendant;

IT IS HEREBY ORDERED AND ADJUDGED THAT:

1. The Plaintiff recover judgment from the Defendant in the sum of $[Amount].

2. The Plaintiff is awarded interest from the Defendant in the sum of $[Amount].

3. The Plaintiff is awarded costs of this action, including all reasonable disbursements, no limiting rule to apply.

_____

J. C. Q. B. A.

APPROVED AS TO ORDER GIVEN:

_____

Solicitors for the Defendant

7

NEGOTIATIONS
AND SETTLEMENT

o Legal counsel should enter into negotiations for the purposes of exploring settlement at any opportunity.

o Such negotiations are "without prejudice" and therefore all
statements made and any documentation which is ex-
changed is inadmissible and without prejudice to the
parties' official position at trial.

7.1   AREAS TO COVER ON BEHALF OF
THE EMPLOYEE

o In negotiating a settlement on behalf of the employee, the
following areas should be covered in the negotiations:
  o The amount;
  o Whether any previous amounts paid to the employee
  should be deducted;
  o Allocation to heads of damage and legal costs:
    o pay in lieu of reasonable notice;
    o interest;
    o reimbursement for legal costs;
    o general damages[1];

---

[1]   Where unemployment benefit repayment is involved, this will be minimized where
the maximum amounts are allocated to legal costs, interest and general damages.
However, only a "retiring allowance" for loss of employment can be rolled over to an
R.R.S.P.

- o tax structuring;
- o pension;
- o benefits continuance or compensation;
- o unemployment benefit repayment obligations and responsibility;
- o letter of reference and reference checks;
- o interest in timing of payment;
- o trust conditions enclosing documentation.

7.2 AREAS TO COVER ON BEHALF OF THE EMPLOYER

- o In negotiating on behalf of the employer, the negotiation should cover the following areas:
  - o amount;
  - o identifying clearly the different components of the damages and the allocation of the agreed settlement. The final settlement amount should be all-inclusive of damages, interest and costs. If not, those amounts should be ascertained before final instructions for settlement are obtained;
  - o Whether any previous payments (i.e., statutory pay in lieu of notice) should be deducted;
  - o The amounts that will be subject to statutory deductions;
  - o Whether the payment is conditional regardless of mitigation or alternative employment;
  - o General release;
  - o Requirement of confidentiality;
  - o Letter of reference and reference checks.

7.3 TIMING AND CONDUCT OF NEGOTIATIONS

7.3.1 REPRESENTING THE EMPLOYEE

- o Negotiations should be fully explored prior to undertaking litigation.

- o It is often helpful to conduct further negotiations just prior to the commencement of examination for discovery in the presence of the other counsel and their client. This is particularly helpful where the client has obtained alternative employment and the damages can be calculated with some degree of precision.

o Further negotiation should take place once the employee has obtained alternative employment taking into consideration the amount of compensation and the benefits in the new job.

o Following examination for discovery, consideration should be given to setting out the employee's offer in a "without prejudice" letter briefly articulating the legal principles and relevant facts in support of the settlement proposal.

o Further negotiations should be considered just prior to trial.

7.3.2 REPRESENTING THE EMPLOYER

o In some cases it is advantageous to negotiate early, in other cases, it is better to negotiate later.

(a) Early Negotiation

o This is advantageous where there is no cause and the employee is entitled to a substantial period of reasonable notice, and has not yet been frustrated through an arduous search for new employment.

o If the employee is reasonably optimistic about locating alternative employment, he or she may be prepared to accept a compromised settlement amount if it is offered shortly after the termination of employment and is fair under the circumstances.

o In any dispute where cause is an issue, it may be advantageous to negotiate early where the employee is prepared to recognize some responsibility for loss of employment.

o In such cases, counsel may wish to insist that no further settlement discussions take place until new employment has been obtained or the period of reasonable notice has run its course.

o Alternatively, the parties may agree on a settlement amount structured as follows:

   o A lump sum payment;
   o Periodic payments until new employment is obtained;
   o Benefits continuance or compensation for loss of benefits until new employment is obtained;
   o A bonus representing a percentage of the unpaid amounts if new employment is obtained before the periodic payments are exhausted.

o Alternatively, the agreed settlement could include continued compensation and benefits until new employment is obtained.

o It may be advantageous to negotiate early where the employee is prepared to accept some responsibility for the loss of employment and is prepared to accept a compromised settlement amount as a result. This can avoid a long, drawn-out and emotionally intense legal battle.

(b)   Later Negotiations

o In wrongful dismissal litigation, it may be advantageous for the employer to negotiate later where the employee is entitled to a substantial period of reasonable notice and the job prospects of alternative employment are reasonably good. The effect of litigation may substantially reduce the damages under the circumstances.

o In such cases, counsel may wish to insist that no further settlement discussions take place until new employment has been obtained or the period of reasonable notice has run its course.

o Alternatively, the parties may agree on a settlement amount structured as follows:

   o A lump sum payment;

   o Periodic payments until new employment is obtained;

   o Benefits continuance or compensation for loss of benefits until new employment is obtained;

   o A bonus representing a percentage of the unpaid amounts if new employment is obtained before the periodic payments are exhausted.

o Alternatively, the agreed settlement could include continued compensation and benefits until new employment is obtained.

7.4 OFFERS OF SETTLEMENT/JUDGMENT

o Where informal settlement discussions are not fruitful, parties should seriously consider filing formal offers of settlement or judgment.

7.4.1 OFFER OF SETTLEMENT

o Rule 170 of the Alberta *Rules of Court* provides that the plaintiff may file and serve an offer of settlement at any time after a statement of defence has been filed.

o The offer must remain open for 45 days after service and then can be withdrawn by filing a notice of withdrawal.

o If the offer is not accepted, and the plaintiff recovers the amount stipulated in the offer or more through litigation, the court will award double party and party costs, except in very rare cases where a substantial reason is accepted by the court as to why double costs should not be awarded (see: R. 174).

o Where the defendant accepts the offer of settlement, negotiations may be entered into for the allocation of the settlement amounts, tax structuring and other matters in order to resolve a claim. If agreement cannot be reached, judgment may be entered for the settlement amount. (See: Appendix 7A – Offer of Settlement – Employee.)

7.4.2   OFFER OF JUDGMENT

o Rule 169 of the Alberta *Rules of Court* allows a defendant to file an offer of judgment stipulating an amount that the defendant is prepared to offer to the plaintiff.

o The offer of judgment should clearly stipulate the amount for damages, pre-judgment interest and costs. Where pre-judgment interests and costs are not set out in monetary amounts, these may be stipulated as additional paragraphs in the offer and calculated upon acceptance.

o Pre-judgment interest will continue to accrue until the offer of judgment has been accepted.

o If it is intended that the plaintiff sign a full and final release as a condition of the offer, that should be stipulated and the form of release should be attached as a schedule to the offer. Otherwise the plaintiff would be in a position to accept the offer and move for judgment without having to sign the release.

o In any event, even without that conditional stipulation the issues related to the litigation would be subject to a defence of accord and satisfaction.

o The offer of judgment must remain open for 45 days after which it may be withdrawn by a notice of withdrawal.

o Where the plaintiff fails to recover more than the amount set out in the offer judgment, the employer will be entitled to its party in party costs in defending against the action from the date that the offer was served (see: R. 174(1)). This advantage applies even where the offer has been withdrawn after the stipulated 45-day time limit.

o Counsel should consider arranging a settlement meeting after the offer of settlement/judgment has been made in order to fully explore the possibility of settlement.

o Where counsel is concerned that the merits of the offer are not clearly being communicated to the other side, arrangements can be considered to include legal counsel and their client.

APPENDIX 7A
Offer of Settlement – Employee

Court Form

IN THE COURT OF QUEEN'S BENCH OF ALBERTA
JUDICIAL CENTRE OF *

B E T W E E N:

[Name]

Plaintiff

- and -

[Name]

Defendant

OFFER TO SETTLE

PURSUANT to Rule 170 of the Alberta *Rules of Court*, the Plaintiff hereby offers to fully and finally settle this action on the following terms:

1. The Defendant shall pay to the Plaintiff the all inclusive sum of $[Amount] for general damages, special damages and interest; and

2. The Defendant shall pay the Plaintiff's taxable costs and disbursements.

PURSUANT to Rule 170(5), if this Offer is not accepted or if a confession of judgment is not filed within 45 days of the date of service, this Offer may be withdrawn by the Plaintiff by serving a Notice of Withdrawal on the Defendant.

PURSUANT to Rule 174(2), if the Plaintiff recovers a sum equal to or greater than the amount of this Offer the judge or the Court of Appeal shall, unless for special reason, award the Plaintiff double the amount of costs (excluding disbursements) he would otherwise have recovered for all steps in relation to the claim after the service of this offer.

DATED at the [City/Town] of [Place], in the Province of Alberta, this [Date].

NAME OF LAW FIRM

Per: _____

Solicitors for the Plaintiff

TO: **NAME OF LAW FIRM**
Solicitors for the Plaintiff

222

APPENDIX 7B
Offer of Judgment – Employer

1. Court Form

IN THE COURT OF QUEEN'S BENCH OF ALBERTA
JUDICIAL CENTRE OF *

B E T W E E N:

[Name]

Plaintiff

- and -

[Name]

Defendant

OFFER OF JUDGMENT

Pursuant to Rule 169 of the Alberta *Rules of Court*, the Defendant hereby offers judgment to the Plaintiff as follows:

1. The sum of $[Amount] for damages, general and special, inclusive of pre-judgment interest pursuant to the *Judgment Interest Act*, R.S.A. 1980, c. J-0.5; and

2. Taxable costs and disbursements.

Pursuant to Rule 169(3), if no acceptance has been filed, the Defendant may, by serving notice of withdrawal upon the Plaintiff, withdraw the offer at any time after 45 days from service of the offer.

Pursuant to Rule 174(1), if the Plaintiff does not recover a sum greater than the amount of this offer, the Judge or the Court of Appeal shall, unless for special reason, award costs to the Defendant for all steps in relation to that claim after the service of notice of this offer.

Dated at the [City/Town] of [Place], in the Province of Alberta this [Date].

NAME OF LAW FIRM

Per: _____
Solicitors for the Defendant

TO: **NAME OF LAW FIRM**
Solicitors for the Plaintiff

223

2. Letter to Employee's Counsel

Lawyer's Name
Direct Line: *
Our File No.: *

[Date]

BY FAX (Original by Mail)
"WITHOUT PREJUDICE"

[Address of Employee's Counsel]

Dear [Sir/Madam]:

Re: *

We have now heard from the Board of Directors of [Name of Employer] regarding this matter. Our most recent offer was for the all-inclusive sum of $[Amount] in full and final settlement of [Name of Employee]'s claims. Your client has made a counter-proposal for the all-inclusive sum of $[Amount] in full and final settlement of [His/Her] claims. We regret to advise that your client's counter-proposal is unacceptable. However, we do have authority to split the difference between our respective offers and are prepared to offer the all-inclusive sum of $[Amount] (less statutory deductions) in full and final settlement. The payment is conditional upon execution of a full and final release in favour of our client, including agreement to a non-disclosure provision. Please advise us as to whether this offer is acceptable to your client.

If the offer is unacceptable, we are prepared to admit service of your client's Statement of Claim and will undertake to file a Statement of Defence in due course. Upon issuance of a Statement of Claim this offer will be automatically withdrawn. We look forward to receiving your client's reply.

Yours very truly,

NAME OF LAW FIRM

Lawyer's Name

cc [Name of Employer]
Attention: [Name of Officer]

APPENDIX 7C
General Release

RELEASE

1. IN CONSIDERATION of payment to me by * in the amount of [amount] Dollars ($[amount]), less sums required by law to be withheld, receipt of which is hereby acknowledged, I, [name], do for myself and my heirs, executors, administrators and assigns, (hereinafter collectively referred to as "I"), forever release, remise and discharge *, its subsidiaries and affiliates and all its officers, directors, employees, agents, insurers and assigns (hereinafter collectively referred to as the "Company"), jointly and severally from any and all actions, causes of actions, contracts, (whether express or implied), claims and demands for damages, loss, or injury, suits, debts, sums of money, indemnity, expenses, interest, costs and claims of any and every kind and nature whatsoever, at law or in equity, which against the Company, I ever had, now have, or can hereafter have by reasons of or existing out of any causes whatsoever existing up to and inclusive of the date of this Release, including but without limiting the generality of the foregoing:

- my employment with the Company;

- the termination of my employment with the Company; and

- any and all claims for damages, salary, wages, termination pay, severance pay, vacation pay, commissions, bonuses, expenses, allowances, incentive payments, insurance or any other benefits arising out of my employment with the Company.

2. NO ADMISSION

I acknowledge that the payment given to me pursuant to the above paragraph does not constitute any admission of liability by or on behalf of the Company.

3. INDEMNITY FOR TAXES, ETC.

I further agree that, for the aforesaid payment, I will save harmless and indemnify the Company from and against all claims, taxes or penalties and demands, which may be made by the Minister of National Revenue requiring the Company to pay income tax under the *Income Tax Act* (Canada) in respect of income tax payable by myself in excess of the income tax previously withheld; and in respect of any and all claims, charges, taxes, or penalties and demands which may be made on behalf of or related to the Canada Employment and Immigration Commission or the Canada Pension Commission under the applicable statutes and regulations, with respect to any amount which may, in the future, be found to be payable by the Company in respect of myself.

4. EMPLOYMENT STANDARDS

I acknowledge receipt of all wages, overtime pay, vacation pay, general holiday pay, and pay in place of termination of employment that I am entitled to by virtue of the *Employment Standards Code* or pursuant to any other labour standards legislation and I further confirm that there are no entitlements, overtime pay or wages due and owing to myself by the Company.

5. BENEFITS AND INSURANCE CLAIMS

I acknowledge and agree that the payment to me includes full compensation and consideration for loss of employment benefits and that all of my employment benefits have ceased on the date of termination of my employment. I acknowledge that I have received all benefit entitlements, including insurance benefits to date, and have no further claim against the Company for benefits. I fully accept sole responsibility to replace those benefits that I wish to continue and to exercise conversion privileges where applicable with respect to benefits. In the event that I become disabled, I covenant not to sue the Company for insurance or other benefits, or for loss of benefits. I hereby release the Company from any further obligations or liabilities arising from my employment benefits.

6. NON-DISCLOSURE

I agree that I will not divulge or disclose, directly or indirectly, the contents of this Release or the terms of settlement relating to the termination of my employment with the Company to any person, including but without limiting the generality of the foregoing, to employees or former employees of the Company, except my legal and financial advisors on the condition that they maintain the confidentiality thereof, or as required by law.

7. CONFIDENTIALITY

I recognize and acknowledge that during my employment with the Company I had access to certain confidential and proprietary information, the disclosure of which could be harmful to the interests of the Company. I acknowledge and agree that I have taken and will in future take appropriate precautions to safeguard the Confidential Information of the Company. Further, I agree that I will respect and abide by any Employee Confidentiality or Assignment of Rights Agreements that I have executed.

8. FURTHER CLAIMS

I agree not to make claim or take proceedings against any other person or corporation that might claim contribution or indemnity under the provisions of any statute or otherwise against the Company.

9. UNDERSTANDING

AND I HEREBY DECLARE that I have had the opportunity to seek independent legal advice with respect to the matters addressed in this Release and the terms of settlement which have been agreed to by myself and the Company and that I fully understand this Release and the terms of settlement. I have not been influenced by any representations or statements made by or on behalf of the Company. I hereby voluntarily accept the said terms for the purpose of making full and final compromise, adjustment and settlement of all claims as aforesaid.

10. COMPLETE AGREEMENT

I understand and agree that this Release contains the entire agreement between the Company and I and that the terms of this Release are contractual and not a mere recital.

DATED at the [City/Town] of [Place], in the Province of Alberta, this ____ day of _____, 199_.

_____

_____
WITNESS [Name]

APPENDIX 7D
Letter to Employer's Counsel Enclosing
Settlement Documents

Lawyer's Name
Direct Line: *
Our File No.: *

[Date]

[Address of Employer's Counsel]

Dear *:

Re: *

Further to your letter of *, we confirm settlement of *'s claims and in that regard we enclose the following:

• Release duly executed by our client;

• A copy of the Notice of Overpayment from Canada Employment and Immigration;

• A copy of letter from Canada Employment and Immigration subsequent to the Statement of Overpayment;

• An executed Discontinuance of Action.

We confirm that there will be no R.R.S.P. rollover deducted.

The within documents are forwarded to you on the trust condition and no use be made of them until such time as the settlement funds, being allocated as $* to legal costs and $* retiring allowance, be paid out in full as follows:

1. That funds in the sum of $* be paid to Canada Employment and Immigration pursuant to the Notice of Overpayment;

2. Your firm's trust cheque for legal costs in the sum of $* be forwarded to this office in trust for our client;

3. Your firm's trust cheque for the balance of the settlement funds, less withholding tax, be forwarded to this office in trust for our client.

Once the above trust conditions have been satisfied, you are at liberty to file the Discontinuance of Action. Please provide us with a filed copy in due course. You are also then at liberty to forward the general release to your client.

I appreciate your co-operation and professional courtesy throughout.

Yours very truly,

NAME OF LAW FIRM

Lawyer's Name

enclosures
cc *

8

PREPARATION FOR TRIAL

8.1 PRE-TRIAL CONFERENCE

- o In cases where the trial is set for three days or longer, a pre-trial conference is mandatory (see: *Alberta Rules of Court*, Civil Practice Note 3 – Pre-trial Conference). In other cases, a pre-trial conference may be scheduled at the request of any party (Alberta *Rules of Court,* R. 219).

- o The purpose of the pre-trial conference before a judge is to:
  - o Ensure counsel are ready for trial;
  - o Explore areas for the possibility of settlement and encourage settlement;
  - o Narrow the issues for trial;
  - o Make suggestions to expedite the trial process;
  - o Admissions of fact and documents;
  - o Agreement as to damages;
  - o Agreement as to legal issues and authorities.

- o Keeping the purposes of the pre-trial conference in mind, counsel should take maximum advantage of this opportunity.

- o Thorough preparation will enable legal counsel to respond to the trial judge, respond to the position of the opposing party, and advance or expedite their client's case through the pre-trial process.

- o Following the pre-trial conference, a report should be prepared for the client which includes an outline of the suggestions of the pre-trial conference judge.

o The pre-trial conference judge will usually forward a report to be submitted to the judge assigned to the trial. He will ask counsel to review the report and sign it.

o A copy of this report should be provided to the client.

o Counsel should then follow up with all of the pre-trial judge's suggestions.

8.2   NOTICE OF TRIAL AND LETTER TO CLIENT

o Once the trial coordinator's office provides you with a notice of trial, send a copy of the notice to your client and all witnesses with a letter outlining the trial process and scheduled times for trial preparation. (See: Appendix 8A – Letter to Plaintiff re Trial; Appendix 8B – Letter to Employer re Trial; Appendix 8C – Letter to Witnesses re Trial).

8.3   EMPLOYEE'S PREPARATION

o The plaintiff should be well-prepared for trial. A great deal of this preparation can be done without any additional legal expense. At a minimum it should include:
  o Review of the letter on the trial process;
  o Review of the producible documents;
  o Review of transcript from examinations for discovery;
  o Notes and comments on other party's examinations;
  o Comments on own testimony;

o Just prior to trial, meet with legal counsel to review the evidence and prepare for trial.

8.4   EMPLOYER'S PREPARATION

o Ensure availability of all employer's witnesses, including former employees and third-party witnesses, and arrange for their preparation by legal counsel just prior to trial.

o Provide the letter on the trial process to all employer witnesses.

o With the assistance of legal counsel, prepare document brief for each particular witness and have the witness review those documents.

o Review the transcripts from the examination for discovery. This should be done by all key witnesses on behalf of the employer.

o Particular parts of the examination for discovery that pertain to that witness should be reviewed and comments should be made.

o Arrange to meet with legal counsel just prior to the trial to review evidence-in-chief and potential evidence of cross-examination.

8.5 WITNESSES AND PREPARATION

o At the time that the notice of trial is received, counsel should turn his or her mind to the witness who will be required to testify at trial.

o The witnesses should be contacted to confirm their availability for the trial date, and provided with the letter and a copy of the notice of trial (see: Appendix 8C – Letter to Witnesses re Trial).

o Send copies of relevant documents and excerpts from the examination for discovery which relate to that witness' testimony.

o Meet with or contact the witness by telephone in order to review those aspects of the evidence.

o Prepare detailed outlines of the evidence-in-chief consisting of the questions to be asked and a summary of the responses. Send these in advance to the witnesses for their comments.

o Schedule a preparation session with the witness just prior to the trial to enable a thorough review of the evidence-in-chief and explore potential areas of cross-examination.

o Together with the witness, consider how difficult areas of the examination will be handled.

o Final versions of the evidence-in-chief and a summary of the response should be given to the witness in advance of the trial. This may be reviewed by the witness up to the time of testimony but should not be brought to the courtroom.

o If the witness is not prepared to co-operate with legal counsel, consider whether his or her evidence is crucial.

o If the evidence is crucial, personally serve a notice to attend together with the requisite amount of conduct money.

o The notice to attend should be accompanied with a covering letter explaining to the witness why his or her evidence is required and that it is critical to ensure a fair trial.

o Phone the witness after serving the notice to attend to see if the witness will now co-operate in the pre-trial preparation.

o During the pre-trial preparation of witnesses, obtain work, home and cellular phone numbers in order to contact them at short notice.

o Canvass the witnesses as to their availability during the scheduled trial, estimate when their evidence will be required and make arrangements to contact them so that they will have sufficient time to travel to the courthouse for testimony.

o Advise the witnesses that the trial may settle. If so, they will be contacted by telephone.

o Follow this up with a letter thanking them for their time and information in assisting you to prepare for trial. Indicate that their evidence was very helpful in being able to resolve the matter.

8.6   TRIAL BRIEF

o Counsel should prepare a trial brief, beginning with the closing argument, updating legal briefing, preparation of the examination-in-chief, a summary of the areas of cross-examination, and concluding with the opening argument.

8.6.1   CLOSING ARGUMENT

o Trial preparation should begin by preparing at least an out-line of the closing argument.

o In appropriate cases, preparation of the detailed closing ar-gument will immediately establish the evidence required in order to establish the facts relied upon in the closing argu-ment and the principles of legal authority needed.

o Ensure that all factual submissions have been dealt with in the evidence and that all legal submissions are supported by legal authority.

o In appropriate cases, a closing argument can be drafted as a working document and refined during the course of the trial.

8.6.2   LEGAL BRIEFING

o Update legal briefing on the issues and review recent cases on the length of reasonable notice under the circumstances of the case at bar.

o Obtain copies of the relevant cases.

o In regard to the appropriate length of reasonable notice, consider assembling a table of cases from a database consisting of the legal citation, age, length of service, salary, period of unemployment, and the period of reasonable notice awarded.

8.6.3   WITNESS QUESTIONS

o After preparing the examination-in-chief and summary of the evidence, place these in the trial brief.

o As each witness is prepared, make rough notes in the margins in order to revise the questions for examination-in-chief prior to trial.

8.6.4   CROSS-EXAMINATION

o Give careful consideration to areas that will require cross-examination.

o Where cause is in issue, this would normally include:
   o Evaluations;
   o Discipline;
   o Counselling sessions and warnings;
   o Job performance;
   o Incidents and all details;
   o Key documents.

o In any case, cross-examination should include:
   o Stature of the plaintiff's position;
   o Notice or severance offered;
   o Compensation and benefits;
   o Mitigation;
   o Details regarding alternative employment;
   o Income received following termination of employment.

o With each witness anticipated to be called by the other side, review the examination for discovery transcripts of that witness and all documents that he or she can speak to.

o Anticipate fruitful areas of cross-examination that will advance your client's case.

o General rule of cross-examination: keep the cross-examination brief and to the point.

o Only cross-examine where there is disputed evidence.

o In areas of evidence that were not covered in examination-in-chief but are critical to your client's case, cross-examine to emphasize significant points.

o Only ask a question through cross-examination if you know the answer, or that the particular answer which is given will not be detrimental to your client's case.

o Where the trial witness was examined for discovery, rely on the examination for discovery transcript as a basis for cross-examination.

8.6.5 READ-INS

o The examination for discovery of a party or an officer on behalf of a corporate party is binding on that party. The questions and answers can therefore be read in at trial by the party who conducted the examination.

o By reading in the examination for discovery, it becomes part of the evidence at trial.

o Where an employee or an agent is examined, the answers must be adopted by the company or be admitted as the information of the company before the questions and answers can be read in.

o Review the examination for discovery transcript and highlight those portions that you wish to read in.

o It may be helpful to the court to reproduce the read-in with the relevant documents tabbed behind so that the judge can follow along.

o The plaintiff usually reads-in from the defendant's discovery after he or she has called all of his or her witnesses and prior to closing the plaintiff's case.

o The defendant usually reads-in after all of the defendant's witnesses and just before the defendant closes its case.

o If the defendant has put the discovery evidence to the plaintiff through cross-examination, there may be no reason to read it in at a later point in the trial.

o Counsel may object to any evidence to be read-in based upon the principles of the law of evidence.

o Where evidence which is read in is taken out of context, the opposing counsel may request that certain additional portions of the transcript be read in to explain or provide the context for the evidence.

8.6.6   OPENING

o The last thing to prepare is the opening statement.

o The opening statement should be brief.

o In the case of the plaintiff, it should identify the issues for trial and provide a brief sketch of the evidence to be presented.

o The defendant may make an opening statement immediately following the plaintiff's opening. Alternatively, the defendant may reserve the opening until the plaintiff has closed its case.

o In a wrongful dismissal action, the defendant usually does not make an opening statement, as the issues and the evidence are relatively clear to the trial judge following the Plaintiff's case.

8.7   ADMISSION OF FACTS AND DOCUMENTS

8.7.1   ADMISSION OF AGREED FACTS

o Counsel should endeavour to admit facts and documents that are not in dispute in order to expedite and simplify the trial process.

o Draft an agreed statement of facts outlining those facts that you would be prepared to admit if you were counsel for the opposite party.

o In a wrongful dismissal suit the following should be readily admitted in most cases:

  o Employment;
  o Dates of service;
  o Termination of employment;
  o Duties and responsibilities;
  o Compensation and benefits;
  o Where cause is not an issue, that the employee was dismissed without cause.

o Once drafted, send the statement of agreed facts to the opposing counsel for comment.

o Finalize the statement, taking into consideration the comments of the opposing counsel.

o If the opposing counsel will not agree to certain facts which should readily be admitted, serve a notice to admit facts under R. 230 of the Alberta *Rules of Court.*

o The opposing counsel will then have 15 days to object to those facts that he or she is not prepared to admit.

o If the facts are ultimately proven at trial, the other party will be required to bear out the costs of calling that evidence (see: R. 230(4)).

8.7.2   DOCUMENTS

o Review all of the documents and identify those that you will be relying on at trial.

o Send a list of those documents and ask the opposing counsel to review the list and advise whether he or she wishes to introduce any other documents at the trial.

o Once the list has been finalized, endeavour to reach the following agreement with respect to the documents: "Parties agree that the following documents are admissible without further proof as evidence at large, for the truth of their contents. However, either party may call further evidence to expand upon, explain, contradict or refute the content of the documents so admitted."

o Alternatively, if the other party is not prepared to admit to the truth of the document, it may be prepared to admit that the document was created on or about its date, sent, and received.

o Where the parties are unable to reach agreement regarding certain documents, these will have to be proven in the normal course at trial.

o Counsel should consider using a notice to admit under R. 230 of the Alberta *Rules of Court* to lay the evidential foundation for documents which are not admitted by agreement. See: Appendix 8E – Notice to Admit – Facts and Documents.

APPENDIX 8A
Letter to Plaintiff re Trial

Lawyer's Name
Direct Line: *
Our File No.: *

[Date]

[Employee's Name and Address]

Dear *:

Re:*

We enclose a copy of the notice from the Alberta Attorney General (Civil Trial Coordinator) advising that your action has now been set for trial for * days, commencing on *. Please ensure that * is available at that time.

We have also written to [Witness' Name] advising him of the trial date, and have requested that he make himself available at that time. A copy of that letter is enclosed.

We are in the process of scheduling the pre-trial conference in this matter and will ensure that it has been held prior to *. We will report to you in that regard in due course.

As the trial date approaches, we will advise you in detail as to the trial process and will make the necessary arrangements to prepare you and the expert witness for the upcoming trial.

Yours very truly,

LAW FIRM NAME

Lawyer's Name

enclosures

Lawyer's Name
Direct Line: *
File No.: *

[Date]

DELIVERED BY COURIER

[Address of Client]

Dear *:

Re:*

As you are aware, we attended a Pre-Trial Conference on [Date] before [Mr./Mde.] Justice [Name] of the Alberta Court of Queen's Bench. It appears that this action is now heading for Trial. For your information, enclosed is a memorandum pertaining to the Pre-Trial Conference which has been prepared by the presiding Judge. That report will now be submitted to the Trial Judge.

You might be interested to know that at the Pre-Trial Conference, [Mr./Mde.] Justice [Name] guessed that the applicable period of reasonable notice might be between * and * months. Interestingly, both the opposing counsel and I suggested that an award in the nature of * months would be more appropriate in your case. I do not believe Justice [Name]'s quick assessment is supported by the bulk of the decisions involving persons of your seniority and length of service. However, it is largely a discretionary matter and varies from judge to judge. That is one of the uncertainties of litigation.

To date, your Offer of Settlement is still outstanding and will be automatically withdrawn at the commencement of Trial. Please advise us at your earliest convenience as to whether you wish us to withdraw the Offer of Settlement. There is no downside to this given that you will still be entitled to double costs if you recover the same or better than the offer at Trial.

The Trial is scheduled to commence at [Date] at [Time] as indicated in the Notice. A copy of the Notice is enclosed for your information. Please advise [Name of Witness] of the date and that we will anticipate calling his evidence on [Date] in the [Fore/After]noon. If you have any difficulty securing [Name of Witness]'s co-operation, please advise me and I will serve him with a Notice to Attend (Subpoena).

I should like to meet with you and [Name of Witness] on [Day], [Date] commencing at [Time] in order to prepare for Trial. I will begin with [Name of Witness] so that he can carry on with his business after that preparation. I anticipate that we will be about one hour with him. As for your preparation, I think that we will be involved for most of the morning and would be delighted to take you to lunch over the lunch hour.

The following is an explanation of the trial process to enable you to better understand the procedure involved and the roles of the participants.

Our system of justice is adversarial – each side is given the opportunity to present its case as best it can by calling witnesses, producing documents, and so forth. Each witness who is called may be cross-examined by the other side, who will try to uncover any weakness or inconsistency in the evidence presented, and bring out the points that they wish to make. Do not take the other lawyer's questions or comments personally. He or she is merely performing their duties in much the same way as I am.

It is your duty at trial to answer all the questions put to you as truthfully and accurately as you can. Do not try to memorize your answers as it is important for you to be sincere. At our pre-trial meeting, I will sit down with you to discuss certain areas of questioning, and together we will review the documents you have provided me.

My function at trial is to organize the evidence and to present it in the most favourable light. This is done in part by calling witnesses, examining them, and cross-examining the witnesses called by the other side. At the end of the case, I will make submissions on your behalf. You must understand, however, that I cannot change sworn evidence or give evidence myself. The best I can do is emphasize the positive aspects of your case, and try to bring out the weaknesses and inconsistencies in the evidence of the other side.

It is the function of the judge to hear the witnesses called by each side and decide which facts are likely to be true. Often, a judge has to make findings of credibility in order to determine what facts actually occurred. If the judge does not believe your evidence, you will almost certainly lose your case. There is precious little a lawyer can do for you under such circumstances. If it is any consolation, such an adverse finding of credibility does not necessarily mean that the judge thinks the witness is lying. Rather, the judge is simply reconciling the conflicting evidence as best he or she can.

Throughout the trial, the other lawyer and I will be making legal submissions to the judge. Sometimes the arguments will be very brief, such as where I object to a question being asked of a witness. Sometimes the arguments can be quite lengthy. When a judge disagrees with a lawyer, it does not mean the case has been prejudged or that the judge dislikes the lawyer or the client. All it means is that, in the judge's opinion, a certain submission or argument is wrong. Even though the judge or opposing counsel may appear irritated by certain arguments, I must make the submissions in any event to ensure that you have a fair trial.

The trial is intended to be a dignified proceeding. No matter how the other side acts, we will conduct ourselves in a restrained and respectful manner. Although it may feel stiff and unnatural, it is important to show that we take the proceedings seriously and respect the dignity of the court. "Sir" or "Madam" is an acceptable form of addressing the judge. Please address him or her appropriately for court.

The trial is usually conducted in the following order:

1. Preliminary matters.

2. Plaintiff's opening statement.

3. Defendant's opening statement (unless deferred or waived).

4. Examination-in-chief of Plaintiff's witnesses, followed by cross-examination by the Defendant of each witness.

5. Read-ins from Examinations for Discovery;

6. Examination-in-chief of the Defendant's witnesses, followed by cross-examination by the Plaintiff of each witness.

7. Plaintiff's closing argument.

8. Defendant's closing argument.

9. Plaintiff's reply.

There may be some variation of this, depending on the circumstances of the case.

In addition to your evidence, the following is a complete list of the witnesses that we will be calling on your behalf:

[Name of Witness(s)]

Please contact us immediately if there are any other witnesses that you feel should be included.

We assume that you have contacted the witnesses, advised them of the trial date and have made arrangements for them to be available for pre-trial preparation.

If you are having any difficulty, please contact us immediately and we will forward a letter, a Notice to Attend (Subpoena) and we will make arrangements for the witness to attend at court. We will try and make this as convenient as possible.

After the judge has heard all of the evidence and the submissions of counsel, he or she will make a decision right on the spot, or reserve the matter for decision until another time. This decision is called a "judgment" and is final, subject only to rights of appeal. If the judge reserves the decision, it is very difficult for us to predict when the judge will grant the decision. He or she has the option of reconvening the court in order to read the judgment out or giving us a written decision.

I hope that this letter assists you in preparing for the trial. I look forward to meeting with you and the other witnesses prior to trial. In the event that you have any questions or concerns before then, please feel free to call.

Yours very truly,

LAW FIRM NAME

Lawyer's Name

APPENDIX 8B
Letter to Employer re Trial

Lawyer's Name
Direct Line: *
Our File No.: *

[Date]

[Employer's Name and Address]

Dear *:

Re:*

We enclose a copy of the notice from the Alberta Attorney General (Civil Trial Coordinator) advising that [Employee's Name]'s action has now been set for trial for * days, commencing on *. Please ensure that * is available at that time.

We have also written to [Witness' Name] advising him of the trial date, and have requested that he make himself available at that time. A copy of that letter is enclosed.

We are in the process of scheduling the pre-trial conference in this matter and will ensure that it has been held prior to *. We will report to you in that regard in due course.

As the trial date approaches, we will advise you in detail as to the trial process and will make the necessary arrangements to prepare you and the expert witness for the upcoming trial.

Yours very truly,

LAW FIRM NAME

Lawyer's Name

enclosures

Lawyer's Name
Direct Line: *
File No.: *

[Date]

DELIVERED BY COURIER

[Address of Client]

Dear *:

Re:*

As you are aware, we attended a Pre-Trial Conference on [Date] before [Mr./Mde.] Justice [Name] of the Alberta Court of Queen's Bench. It appears that this action is now heading for Trial. For your information, enclosed is a memorandum pertaining to the Pre-Trial Conference which has been prepared by the presiding Judge. That report will now be submitted to the Trial Judge.

You might be interested to know that at the Pre-Trial Conference, [Mr./Mde.] Justice [Name] guessed that the applicable period of reasonable notice might be between * and * months. I do not believe Justice [Name]'s quick assessment is supported by the bulk of the decisions involving persons of the Plaintiff's seniority and length of service. However, it is largely a discretionary matter and varies from judge to judge. That is one of the uncertainties of litigation.

To date, your Offer of Judgment is still outstanding and will be automatically withdrawn at the commencement of Trial. Please advise us at your earliest convenience as to whether you wish us to withdraw the Offer of Judgment. There is no downside to this given that you will still be entitled to party and party costs if the Plaintiff recovers the same or less than the offer at Trial.

The Trial is scheduled to commence at [Date] at [Time] as indicated in the Notice. A copy of the Notice is enclosed for your information. Please advise [Name of Witness] of the date and that we will anticipate calling his evidence on [Date] in the [Fore/After]noon. If you have any difficulty securing [Name of Witness]'s co-operation, please advise me and I will serve him with a Notice to Attend (Subpoena).

I should like to meet with you and [Name of Witness] on [Day], [Date] commencing at [Time] in order to prepare for Trial. I will begin with [Name of Witness] so that he can carry on with his business after that preparation. I anticipate that we will be about one hour with him. As for your preparation, I think that we will be involved for most of the morning and would be delighted to take you to lunch over the lunch hour.

The following is an explanation of the trial process to enable you to better understand the procedure involved and the roles of the participants.

Our system of justice is adversarial – each side is given the opportunity to present its case as best it can by calling witnesses, producing documents, and so forth. Each witness who is called may be cross-examined by the other side, who will try to uncover any weakness or inconsistency in the evidence presented, and bring out the points that they wish to make. Do not take the other lawyer's questions or comments personally. He or she is merely performing their duties in much the same way as I am.

It is your duty at trial to answer all the questions put to you as truthfully and accurately as you can. Do not try to memorize your answers as it is important for you to be sincere. At our pre-trial meeting, I will sit down with you to discuss certain areas of questioning, and together we will review the documents you have provided me.

My function at trial is to organize the evidence and to present it in the most favourable light. This is done in part by calling witnesses, examining them, and cross-examining the witnesses called by the other side. At the end of the case, I will make submissions on your behalf. You must understand, however, that I cannot change sworn evidence or give evidence myself. The best I can do is emphasize the positive aspects of your case, and try to bring out the weaknesses and inconsistencies in the evidence of the other side.

It is the function of the judge to hear the witnesses called by each side and decide which facts are likely to be true. Often, a judge has to make findings of credibility in order to determine what facts actually occurred. If the judge does not believe your evidence, you will almost certainly lose your case. There is precious little a lawyer can do for you under such circumstances. If it is any consolation, such an adverse finding of credibility does not necessarily mean that the judge thinks the witness is lying. Rather, the judge is simply reconciling the conflicting evidence as best he or she can.

Throughout the trial, the other lawyer and I will be making legal submissions to the judge. Sometimes the arguments will be very brief, such as where I object to a question being asked of a witness. Sometimes the arguments can be quite lengthy. When a judge disagrees with a lawyer, it does not mean the case has been prejudged or that the judge dislikes the lawyer or the client. All it means is that, in the judge's opinion, a certain submission or argument is wrong. Even though the judge or opposing counsel may appear irritated by certain arguments, I must make the submissions in any event to ensure that you have a fair trial.

The trial is intended to be a dignified proceeding. No matter how the other side acts, we will conduct ourselves in a restrained and respectful manner. Although it may feel stiff and unnatural, it is important to show that we take the proceedings seriously and respect the dignity of the court. "Sir" or "Madam" is an acceptable form of addressing the judge. Please address them appropriately for court.

The trial is usually conducted in the following order:

1. Preliminary matters.

2. Plaintiff's opening statement.

3. Defendant's opening statement (unless deferred or waived).

4. Examination-in-chief of Plaintiff's witnesses, followed by cross-examination by the Defendant of each witness.

5. Read-ins from Examinations for Discovery;

6. Examination-in-chief of the Defendant's witnesses, followed by cross-examination by the Plaintiff of each witness.

7. Plaintiff's closing argument.

8. Defendant's closing argument.

9. Plaintiff's reply.

There may be some variation of this, depending on the circumstances of the case.

In addition to your evidence, the following is a complete list of the witnesses that we will be calling on your behalf:

[Name of Witness(s)]

Please contact us immediately if there are any other witnesses that you feel should be included.

We assume that you have contacted the witnesses, advised them of the trial date and have made arrangements for them to be available for pre-trial preparation.

If you are having any difficulty, please contact us immediately and we will forward a letter, a Notice to Attend (Subpoena) and we will make arrangements for the witness to attend at court. We will try and make this as convenient as possible.

After the judge has heard all of the evidence and the submissions of counsel, he or she will make a decision right on the spot, or reserve the matter for decision until another time. This decision is called a "judgment" and is final, subject only to rights of appeal. If the judge reserves the decision, it is very difficult for us to predict when the judge will grant the decision. He or she has the option of reconvening the court in order to read the judgment out or giving us a written decision.

I hope that this letter assists you in preparing for the trial. I look forward to meeting with you and the other witnesses prior to trial. In the event that you have any questions or concerns before then, please feel free to call.

Yours very truly,

LAW FIRM NAME

Lawyer's Name

APPENDIX 8C
Letter to Witnesses re Trial

Lawyer's Name
Direct Line: *
Our File No.: *

[Date]

[Witness' Name and Address]

Dear *:

Re:*

Thank you for agreeing to act as a witness on behalf of [Employee's Name/Employer's Name] in [His/Her/Their] action against [Employee's Name/Employer's Name]. We enclose a copy of the notice from the Alberta Attorney General (Civil Trial Coordinator) advising that the action has now been set for trial for * days, commencing on *. The address of the courthouse is *. Please ensure that you are available at that time.

Court commences at 10AM but I prefer to meet my witnesses at the courthouse one-half hour prior to the start of the trial. Typically, there is a lunch break from 12 noon to 2PM and trials finish at 4PM. I will endeavour to provide you with a more exact date and time of your planned appearance as the trial date approaches.

As this may be your first time appearing in court as a witness, it may prove helpful to provide you with some suggestions of how you should act in court, as well as details of the trial process:

• The purpose of your testimony in the trial is to provide the judge [and jury] with important evidence with which to decide whether the Plaintiff's case is successful or not. It is therefore critical that you speak slowly and clearly to the court so that your testimony can be understand.

• I will examine you first, as you are one of the witnesses in favour of the [Plaintiff/Defendant]. I will ask you a number of broad and open-ended questions and will not be allowed to guide you through any evidence by asking leading questions.

• The opposing counsel will then cross-examine you on your testimony, and possibly the evidence you gave at examination for discovery. [He/She] will attempt to gain admissions from you which are designed to assist their case;

- Understand the questions. If you do not understand, say so. Think before answering. Do not overstate your case. In very few cases will a witness have to use the words "never" or "always".

- Wait for counsel to complete his or her question before you begin to answer it.

- Be approximate concerning figures and distances. You do not have to be exact. *Never* guess.

- Do not be afraid to admit that you do not know or cannot remember something.

- Make your answers brief and direct.

- Do not volunteer anything because it may allow the other counsel a chance to explore something which he had not thought of.

- If I object to a question asked by the opposing counsel, do not answer the question until the judge has made his decision on whether my objection is sustained or not.

- If the judge interrupts counsel or asks you a direct question, stop, listen and provide him or her with the appropriate response.

- Obviously, always tell the truth to the court.

I hope the foregoing tips are helpful and recommend that you become familiar with these points as well as any documents which will refresh your memory about this matter.

I will be in contact with you as the trial draws near. Thank you for your assistance in this matter and please do not hesitate to contact me at the number above if you have any further questions.

Yours very truly,

LAW FIRM NAME

Lawyer's Name

APPENDIX 8D
Lawyers' Preparation Checklist

1. Certificate of Readiness of Record filed and served. ☐

   Date Completed _____

2. Pre-trial conference:

   (i) Scheduled ☐   Date: _____

   (ii) Held ☐   Date: _____

3. Trial date scheduled:

   ☐ Notice of trial.

   ☐ Dates entered: _____

4. Preparation For Trial:

   ☐ Pre-trial preparation schedule completed.

   ☐ Forwarded to client.

   ☐ Forwarded to witnesses.

   ☐ Letter outlining trial process sent to client.

   ☐ Letter to witnesses sent.

   ☐ Witness preparation scheduled.

   ☐ Where applicable, Notice(s) to Attend served together with conduct money.

   ☐ Affidavits of Service filed.

   ☐ Draft closing argument prepared.

   ☐ Legal briefing updated and relevant cases copied.

   ☐ Examination-in-Chief prepared for each witness.

   ☐ List of Witnesses:
       (i)   _____
       (ii)   _____
       (iii) _____
       (iv)   _____
       (v)   _____

   ☐ Cross-examination prepared.

☐ List of opposing party's witnesses anticipated:
    (i)   _____
    (ii)   _____
    (iii)   _____
    (iv)   _____
    (v)   _____

☐ Read-ins prepared.

☐ Opening statement prepared.

☐ Trial brief completed.

☐ Draft agreed statement of facts prepared.

☐ Forwarded to opposing counsel for comment.

☐ Statement of Agreed Facts completed and signed.

☐ Where applicable, Notice to Admit prepared and served where opposing counsel will not readily admit facts and documents.

5. Documents

☐ Documents reviewed and a list prepared of those to be admitted at trial.

☐ List of documents forwarded to the opposing counsel for comment and additions.

☐ List of agreed documents completed.

☐ Wording pertaining to Admission of Documents agreed to and signed.

☐ Final Schedule of agreed documents listed with tab numbers.

☐ Agreed exhibit books assembled, including copies for Clerk, Trial Judge, Opposing Counsel and Client.

☐ Examination-in-Chief questions and Summary of Evidence forwarded to witnesses for comment.

6. Witness preparation:

☐ Name of Witness: _____

☐ Date Scheduled: _____

☐ Preparation Completed: _____

APPENDIX 8E
Notice to Admit – Facts and Documents

IN THE COURT OF QUEEN'S BENCH OF ALBERTA
JUDICIAL CENTRE OF *

BETWEEN:

*

Plaintiff

- and -

*

Defendant

NOTICE TO ADMIT

TAKE NOTICE that you are asked, pursuant to Rule 230, to admit, the following facts, for the purpose of the present lawsuit only:

(a) that the Plaintiff's document [Document Number] is a true copy of the original (photocopy attached herewith as Schedule *);

(b) that the original of the Plaintiff's document * was duly executed on or about its date by the parties named therein;

(c) that the parties to Plaintiff's document * were at all material times *sui juris*;

(d) that the Plaintiff's document * was never revoked or amended, and remained in force at all material times;

(e) that the Plaintiff attempted to speak to * but was refused entrance to [his/her] office.

(f) that the Plaintiff wrote a letter to * explaining the incident on * (photocopy attached herewith as Schedule *);

(g) that the Plaintiff incurred the expenses recited in Schedule * hereto.

AND FURTHER TAKE NOTICE that if you do not reply with reasons within 15 days of service hereof you will be deemed to admit these facts;

AND FURTHER TAKE NOTICE that if you deny any of these matters without good cause, the costs of proving the same at trial may be assessed against you irrespective of the outcome of the trial.

DATED at the [City/Town] of [Place], in the Province of Alberta, this [Date].

LAW FIRM NAME

Per: _____

Solicitors for the Plaintiff

9

THE CONDUCT OF THE TRIAL

9.1 PRELIMINARY MATTERS

o With diligent pre-trial preparation, the conduct of the trial should go relatively smoothly.

o It is a prudent practice to meet your client at your office in order to touch up on some final matters and to arrive comfortably at the court house to allow sufficient time to change, set up the trial briefs, and be ready by the trial's commencement time.

o Prior to the formal commencement of trial, the trial judge may ask counsel to attend at his or her chambers to canvass the possibility of settlement, the anticipated length of the trial, and any other issues of concern.

o Once the formal trial commences, any preliminary matters should be attended to. This may include:
   o Final amendments to pleadings;
   o Introduction of a statement of agreed facts;
   o Introduction of agreed exhibits and providing the trial judge with his or her copy;
   o Obtaining a witness exclusion order, if applicable.

9.2 ORDER OF PROCEEDINGS

o Once the preliminary matters have been attended to, the trial should proceed in the following manner:

  (i) Plaintiff's opening statement;
  (ii) Defendant's opening statement, if desired.

9.2.1 PLAINTIFF'S CASE

o Examination-in-chief of the plaintiff;

o Cross-examination of the plaintiff;

o Examination-in-chief of the plaintiff's other witnesses;

o Cross-examination of the plaintiff's other witnesses;

o Read-ins from defendant's examination for discovery.

9.2.2 DEFENDANT'S CASE

o Defendant's opening, if not previously delivered;

o Examination-in-chief of defendant's witnesses;

o Cross-examination of defendant's witnesses; and

o Read-ins from plaintiff's examination for discovery.

9.2.3 CLOSING ARGUMENT

o Closing argument of plaintiff;

o Closing argument of defendant;

o Reply by plaintiff.

9.2.4 JUDGMENT

o At the conclusion of the trial, the trial judge may deliver a judgment from the bench. In that case, counsel should be prepared to make submissions with respect to costs.

o In many cases, the trial judge will want to reserve judgment and issue a written decision.

o In some cases, the judge may request written argument in order to assist in the clarification of the evidence and the legal submissions.

o It is customary for counsel to shake hands and congratulate each other at the conclusion of the trial.

10

POST-TRIAL MATTERS

10.1 JUDGMENT, COSTS AND INTEREST

10.1.1 PLAINTIFF'S COUNSEL

- o If you are acting for a plaintiff who was successful:
  - o You may be required to speak to costs. If costs are awarded, prepare a bill of costs and forward it to the opposing counsel. If you cannot obtain agreement, proceed immediately to taxation before a taxing officer. (See: Orkin, *The Law of Costs* (2nd ed.) (Canada Law Book, 1996)).
  - o Prepare, file and serve a judgment roll (see: Appendix 10A).
  - o Attempt to reach agreement with the opposing counsel regarding allocation of the judgment and the timing of payment. As to income tax considerations, see: Chapter 11, *infra*.
  - o Judgment interest applies until the judgment is paid in full (see: *Judgment Interest Act*, S.A. 1984, c. J-0.5).
  - o If satisfactory arrangements to pay the judgment, costs and interest are not achieved, then immediately begin execution proceedings. See: Section 10.3 – Collection.
  - o If the defendant appeals, this does not prevent finalizing the bill of costs and does not automatically result in a stay of execution. Execution proceedings can continue unless the defendant obtains a stay of execution pending the appeal.

o If you are acting for a plaintiff who is unsuccessful:

- o Review the judgment and provide a reporting letter to your client critically going through the decision and advising of any potential grounds of appeal.
- o If costs have been awarded to the defendant, advise your client as to his or her liability for costs and determine whether he or she will be in a position to offer payment.
- o A meeting should be arranged with your client as soon as possible to review these matters and to obtain instructions as to an appeal.
- o Counsel may wish to consider approaching the other side to waive costs if the plaintiff is prepared to forego any rights of appeal.

10.1.2   DEFENDANT'S COUNSEL

o If the plaintiff is successful, provide a report to your client advising them of the decision and their liability for judgment, costs and interest.

o Review the bill of costs prepared by the opposing counsel to determine whether the bill of costs is proper and whether there is any basis for an objection.

o Attempt to finalize the bill of costs by agreement, failing which the matter should proceed to taxation. (See: Orkin, *The Law of Costs* (2nd ed.) (Canada Law Book, 1996)).

o Review the judgment roll. If it is proper, sign the judgment roll and return it to the opposing counsel. Once the judgment roll has been served, the defendant has 20 days to file a notice of appeal (see: Alberta *Rules of Court*, R. 506). It is a prudent practice to enter this date into the limitation diary system to ensure that instructions are obtained prior to the expiry of the time limit.

o It is also a prudent practice to arrange a meeting with your client after the judgment has been delivered in order to review the situation and obtain instructions regarding appeal.

o If the defendant is successful:

  o Prepare a bill of costs and forward it to the opposing counsel for approval. If agreement is reached, discuss arrangements with the opposing counsel for payment of the costs. If agreement is not reached, proceed immediately to taxation before the taxing officer.

  o Once the bill of costs has been taxed, prepare a writ of attachment for the costs and proceed to collection proceedings. See: Section 10.3 – Collection.

10.2 STATUTORY DEDUCTIONS

o Moneys collected through a wrongful dismissal judgment are subject to statutory deductions for income tax and repayment obligations of unemployment benefits. See: *Employment Insurance Act*, S.C. 1996, c. 23, ss. 45 and 46; *Income Tax Act*, R.S.C. 1985, c. 1 (5th Supp.), s. 56(1) and (1.1); and Section 2.7.4(a), *supra*.

o Therefore, prior to payment of the judgment, the amount of the judgment and the allocation must be communicated to a Canada Employment and Immigration Centre to determine the amount of overpayment and this amount must be remitted prior to payment to the plaintiff.

o The applicable amount of income tax must be applied to the amount awarded by the court and legal costs arising from the wrongful dismissal claim. See: Chapter 11 – Income Tax Considerations.

o The plaintiff may wish to defer the tax by filing a Revenue Canada TD2 form and rolling all or a portion of the judgment into his or her R.R.S.P. See: Chapter 11 – Income Tax Considerations.

10.3 COLLECTION

o Where agreement cannot be reached with the opposing counsel regarding payment of the outstanding judgment or costs, initiate collection proceedings as soon as possible.

o In Alberta, all collection matters are now covered by the *Civil Enforcement Act*, S.A. 1994, c. C-10.5. For a detailed review of the legislation, see: L.E.S.A., *Civil Enforcement Act* (1995).

o Ensure that a writ of enforcement is filed in the Court of Queen's Bench stipulating the judgment, judgment interest to the date of filing the writ, and costs.

o Register all writs in the Personal Property Registry as well.

o Ensure that the writ of enforcement is updated periodically to add any costs related to the enforcement proceedings.

o Information regarding collection and assistance may be obtained from any number of the privatized collection services. These services are licensed as private bailiffs under the *Civil Enforcement Act*, ss. 9-15.

APPENDIX 10A
Judgment Roll

IN THE COURT OF QUEEN'S BENCH OF ALBERTA
JUDICIAL CENTRE OF *

BEFORE THE HONOURABLE) At the Court House in

) the [City/Town] of

[MR./MADAM] JUSTICE [NAME]) [Place], in the Province of

) Alberta, on

IN CHAMBERS) [Weekday], the [Date].

)

)

[Style of Cause]

JUDGMENT ROLL

THIS ACTION having come on for trial upon this date before the Honourable [Mr./Madam] Justice [Name] at the sittings of [His/Her] Honourable Court held at the [City/Town] of [Place], in the Province of Alberta; AND HAVING read the pleadings herein, and hearing what was adduced by the way of evidence on behalf of the parties hereto, and upon hearing counsel for all parties:

IT WAS HEREBY ORDERED AND ADJUDGED THAT:

1. The Plaintiff [Name] recover from the Defendants the sum of $[Amount].

2. The Plaintiff [Name] recover from the Defendants their costs to be taxed on Column *, no limiting rule to apply, including all reasonable disbursements.

3. The individual Defendants do indemnify the Defendant [Name] against all liability under the judgment herein, and in the event of the Defendant [Name] paying to the Plaintiffs the judgment herein and costs, the Defendant [Name] shall be at liberty to sign judgment against the individual Defendants for the amount of the judgment debt and costs so paid.

4. The Defendant [Name] do recover from the individual Defendants the costs of the Defendant [Name] incurred in defending the action, such costs to be taxed.

_____

Clerk of the Court

265

APPROVED AS TO JUDGMENT GIVEN:

NAME OF LAW FIRM

Per: _____
    Solicitors for the Plaintiffs

NAME OF LAW FIRM

Per: _____
    Solicitors for the Defendants

ENTERED THIS [Date].

_____
Clerk of the Court (Seal)

APPENDIX 10B
Bill of Costs

[Style of Cause]

BILL OF COSTS OF THE PLAINTIFF

ITEM	FEES	DISBURSEMENTS
(Steps Taken to [Date]) **(Column 5)**		
1. Commencement of proceedings by Statement of Claim	$ 120.00	$ 25.00
4. Service of Statement of Claim by registered mail	$ 5.00	$ 2.81
12(a) Examination of opposite parties or witnesses before trial	$ 90.00	$
12(b) Examination of additional opposite party before trial	$ 40.00	$ 125.75
12(c) Attending examination of a party by an opposing party	$ 40.00 $ 40.00	$ 116.75
18. Setting down for trial	$ 15.00	$ 2.00
30. Correspondence necessarily relating to proceedings	$ 70.00	
(Steps Taken after [Date]) **(Double Column 3)**		
23. Admission of Facts	$ 250.00	
24. Preparation for Trial (a) First 2 witnesses briefed (b) Two additional witnesses briefed	$ 400.00 $ 160.00	
26. Counsel fee at Trial (Four full 1/2 days at 2‰ hours) (1/3 of 1/2 day)	$ 130.00 $ 1,600.00	

267

31. Preparation of Bill of Costs $ 120.00

32. Taxation of Bill of Costs where
unopposed $ 40.00

43. Entry of Judgment after Contest $ 200.00
                                                     $ 3,320.00

DISBURSEMENTS:

Paid to [Name of Expert]
re: * Report $ 2,426.19

Paid to [Name of Expert]
re: * Report $ 1,433.00

Conduct Money to [Name] for
attendance at trial $ 45.00

Conduct Money to [Name] for
attendance at trial $ 12.00

Conduct Money to [Name] for
attendance at trial $ 12.00

Paid re: photocopying $ 73.10

Paid re: long distance calls $ 56.77

Paid re: courier deliveries $ 12.00

Paid re: TWX to client $ 10.00
                                                     $4,352.37

TOTAL FEE: $3,320.00
TOTAL DISBURSEMENTS: $4,352.37
TAXED ON/OFF: $ [Amount]
TOTAL: $ [Amount]

The above Bill of Costs has been taxed by me this [Date], at [Place], Alberta, AND ALLOWED AT: $[Amount].

_____
Clerk of the Court

APPROVED AND AGREED TO:

NAME OF LAW FIRM

Per: _____
Solicitors for the Defendants

APPENDIX 10C
Letter to Canada Employment and Immigration Commission
re Overpayment

Lawyer's Name
Direct Line: *
Our File No.: *

[Date]

[Contact Name]
Canada Employment and Immigration
Unit C, 220 - 4th Avenue S.E.
Calgary, Alberta
T2P 2T7

Dear [Sir/Madam]:

Re: [Employee's Name]
S.I.N. *

Further to our recent advice and the settlement of the above matter, we are now in receipt of the Notice of Overpayment of Unemployment Benefits with respect to the above matter, a copy of which is enclosed. We enclose our firm trust cheque in the sum of $[Amount] in payment of our client's over-payment.

Yours very truly,

NAME OF LAW FIRM

Lawyer's Name

enclosure

cc *

cc *

APPENDIX 10D
Satisfaction of Judgment Piece

IN THE COURT OF QUEEN'S BENCH OF ALBERTA
JUDICIAL CENTRE OF *

BETWEEN:

[Name]

Plaintiff

- and -

[Name]

Defendant

SATISFACTION OF JUDGMENT PIECE

SATISFACTION OF THE JUDGMENT in the within action is hereby acknowledged on behalf of the Plaintiff, and the Plaintiff hereby consents to a Memorandum of Satisfaction being endorsed by the Clerk of this Honourable Court.

DATED at the [City/Town] of [Place], in the Province of Alberta, this [Date].

NAME OF LAW FIRM

Per: _____
Solicitors for the Plaintiff

TO: Clerk of the Court

11

INCOME TAX CONSIDERATIONS

11.1 RETIRING ALLOWANCE

- o A "retiring allowance" received after termination of employment includes an amount received in respect of the loss of an office or employment, whether or not received in lieu of damages or whether or not paid pursuant to a court or tribunal order. See: *Income Tax Act* ("*I.T.A.*"), R.S.C. 1985, c. 1 (5th Supp.), s. 248(1).

- o Retiring allowances are brought into the employee taxpayer's income for the year of receipt. See: *I.T.A.*, s. 56(1)(a).

- o Section 153(1)(c) of the *I.T.A.* requires an employer or person paying a retiring allowance to withhold tax and report the payment on Form T4A. This requirement applies to severance payments made upon termination of employment, out-of-court settlements, or an amount paid pursuant to a court order. (See: *Skaarup v. Andover & Perth United Farmers' Co-op. Ltd.* (1987), 77 N.B.R. (2d) 132 (Q.B.), affirmed (1987), 18 C.C.E.L. 63 (C.A.); *Frost v. Montreal Engineering Co.* (1983), 3 C.C.E.L. 86 (Alta. Q.B.)).

- o Certain amounts awarded to a former employee under various heads of damages may not fall within the definition of a "retiring allowance", and are therefore not taxable under s. 56(1)(a)(ii) of the *I.T.A.*.
  - o These may include damages for personal injury or death, regardless of whether such damages are calculated

273

based upon lost wages, are not income and therefore are not taxable, provided that the damages cannot reasonably be regarded as employment income.

o In certain circumstances this could include exemplary and punitive damages, damages for mental distress, or damages for defamation which arise from a tort committed by the former employer rather than termination of an office or employment.

o However, where exemplary damages or damages for mental distress can be attributable to an amount received in respect of the loss of an office or employment, they are properly included in the taxpayer's income as a retiring allowance (see: *Young v. Minister of National Revenue* (1986), [1986] 2 C.T.C. 2111 (T.C.C.)).

o As well, an amount received pursuant to an employment contract, whether received on the termination of employment or otherwise, will be considered to be employment income pursuant to ss. 5(1) and 6 of the *I.T.A.*, and will not be considered to be a retiring allowance.

o In order to be a retiring allowance, the damages or settlement must be attributable to a loss of an office or employment. Therefore, damages in respect of a breach of pre-employment arrangements are not retiring allowances and such payments are not taxable (see: *Richardson v. Minister of National Revenue* (1988), [1988] 1 C.T.C. 2219 (T.C.C.)).

o An amount awarded by a court, or attributable to legal costs, arising from a wrongful dismissal claim, are included in the taxpayer's income.

o However, legal fees and expenses incurred in recovering a retiring allowance are deductible from the settlement or award for wrongful dismissal. They cannot be claimed against other income, nor can they be claimed against income which has been deferred by a rollover to a Registered Retirement Savings Plan (R.R.S.P.). See: *I.T.A.*, ss. 56(1)(l.1) and 60(o.1).

o Where a wrongful dismissal award or settlement includes an amount described as interest, it will be taxable as interest rather than as part of a retiring allowance. See: *Interpretation Bulletin*, IT-396 R, "Interest Income", para. 12.

11.2   TRANSFER TO R.R.S.P.

o An employee who is in receipt of a retiring allowance may avoid payment of withholding tax by transferring all or a portion of the retiring allowance to an R.R.S.P.

o Where an amount is paid as damages to a former employee, the taxpayer is entitled to transfer up to $2,000 for each year of employment until December 31, 1995 in respect of which the retiring allowance has been paid to his or her R.R.S.P., pursuant to s. 60(j.1) of the *I.T.A.*. No amounts are allowed for service after December 31, 1995.

o The employee is also entitled to transfer an additional $1,500 from the retiring allowance to his or her R.R.S.P. for each year of employment before 1989 in respect of which the retiring allowance is being paid, where the employee was not a participant in a pension plan.

o All amounts transferred to an R.R.S.P. pursuant to s. 60(j.1) are deductible from the amount of the retiring allowance, which would otherwise be taxable to the former employee. See: *Interpretation Bulletin*, IT-337R2, para. 14.

o The R.R.S.P. rollover is being gradually eliminated as a result of the February 1995 federal budget. However, it is still available in respect of employment prior to 1996. Therefore, the budget change will reduce but not eliminate the rollover for most employees. See: Harris, *Wrongful Dismissal* (Carswell, 1996), §8.2.

o The prescribed form for reporting and claiming the deferral is Form T2097. See: Revenue Canada's "Pension and R.R.S.P. Tax Guide" and *Interpretation Bulletin*, IT-337R2, paras. 12 and 13.

11.3   EMPLOYER DEDUCTIONS

o An employer is obligated to deduct income tax from a settlement that clearly arises from a loss of office or employment. See: *Fieguth v. Acklands Ltd.* (1989), 59 D.L.R. (4th) 114 (B.C.C.A.); *Schneider v. Electrohome Ltd.*, (February 8, 1990), Bolan L.J.S.C., Doc. Waterloo 199/87 (Ont. H.C.) (*The Lawyer's Weekly* 942-016). For further reference, see: *Interpretation Bulletin*, IT-337R2, "Retiring Allowances".

o The following are the withholding tax amounts based on the following settlement/judgment:

Amount	Witholding Tax (%)
0 to $5,000	10%;
Over $5,000 but less than $15,000	20%;
Over $15,000	30%.

12

APPEAL

12.1 APPEAL CONSIDERATIONS

o Either party may wish to file an appeal where the trial judge committed an error of law or where the findings of fact cannot be reasonably supported by the evidence.

o As long as the trial judge has followed proper legal principles, an appellate court will not likely disturb his or her assessment of reasonable notice.

o The costs of the appeal should be carefully weighed against the benefits:
  o In the case of the employee, the net potential recovery must be weighed against the income tax consequences, legal fees, and any unemployment benefits repayment. As such, the net recovery to the plaintiff may not justify the cost associated with an appeal.
  o In the case of the employer, the additional legal costs must be weighed against the possibility of an appellate court interfering with the trial judge's decision.

12.2 EFFECT OF APPEAL

o A notice of appeal must be filed and served within 20 days of the judgment or judgment roll. See: Alberta *Rules of Court*, R. 506.

o The appeal does not act as a stay of any judgment which was granted by the trial court. See: R. 508.

o In order to obtain a stay, the defendant would have to establish:
  o a serious issue for appeal;
  o irreparable harm;
  o that the balance of convenience favours granting a stay.

12.3   APPEAL PREPARATION

o Following filing and service of the notice of appeal, parties will have to prepare the following pursuant to the Alberta *Rules of Court*:
  o agreement as to the content of the appeal books;
  o arrange for assembly of the appeal books;
  o appellate factums;
  o legal authorities.

o For preparation of appeal books and factums, counsel should refer to RR. 530-543 of the Alberta *Rules of Court*, and the Court of Appeal Consolidated Practice Notes (February, 1991).

o Once factums are filed, an appeal hearing will be scheduled for the next session of the Alberta Court of Appeal.

o Counsel may wish to invite their client to be present during the appeal hearing.

o For further information on appeals, see: Pt. 39 (RR. 501-543) of the Alberta *Rules of Court*.

INDEX